Frank Uit de Weerd and Marita

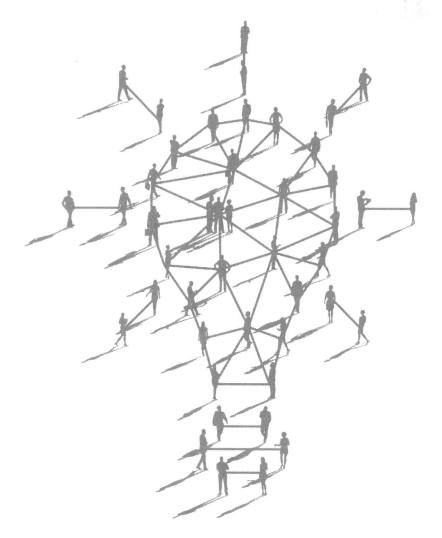

SYSTEMS INSPIRED
LEADERSHIP

How to Tap Collective Wisdom to Navigate Change,
Enhance Agility, and Foster Collaboration

Systems Inspired Leadership

How to Tap Collective Wisdom to Navigate Change, Enhance Agility, and Foster Collaboration

Frank Uit de Weerd and Marita Fridjhon

Published by CRR Global

https://crrglobal.com

ISBN: 978-1-7374976-0-8

Systems Inspired Leadership has been written

through the relationship system of

Frank Uit de Weerd and Marita Fridjhon

PRAISE FOR SYSTEMS INSPIRED LEADERSHIP

To resolve the challenges that face us today, we must shift our attention to our shared human experience, rather than our individual accomplishments. Systems Inspired Leadership provides the tools for doing precisely that in a way that is pragmatic, accessible, and offers a clear road map for those who will lead us into our best future.

KAREN KIMSEY-HOUSE, CO-FOUNDER, THE CO-ACTIVE TRAINING INSTITUTE, AUTHOR OF CO-ACTIVE COACHING, CO-ACTIVE LEADERSHIP, AND INTEGRATION

This timely book equips readers with the essential human skills to lead through the unique qualities and interconnections that emerge from relationship systems we create together. An inspirational must-read packed with practical applications for all leaders who want to enable and empower intentional relationships that will change the world. It has never been more important to be human than now.

DR. CARA ANTOINE, MANAGING DIRECTOR DIGITAL TRANSFORMATION, IG&H

This body of work is a brilliant coalescence of everything I dream of being as a leader, and I believe it is an essential ingredient for unlocking the full potential of people, teams, organizations, and the larger global community. Even if you already feel skillful as a leader and have been studying systems thinking and professional coaching techniques, this book includes models and concepts that will help you dramatically up your game.

LESLIE J. MORSE, PRODUCT OWNER OF THE PROFESSIONAL SCRUM COMMUNITY AT SCRUM.ORG

This brilliant book—insightful, wise, and revolutionary—calls us forth to challenge the traditional leadership worldview and its limitations, expand our perceptions, and awaken our sensibilities. What it promises, it delivers. As a relationship systems practitioner who works with leaders in the resolution of workplace harassment and high conflict, I have witnessed the transformative power of Systems Inspired Leadership time and time again. Steeped in respect for each and every member of a system and committed to creating psychological safety for all, this innovative approach to leadership is precisely what our organizations and institutions need—what we all need—now more than ever.

JENNIFER PERNFUSS, LL.B., LEGALLY TRAINED SYSTEMS INSPIRED WORKPLACE RESTORATION PRACTITIONER AND FOUNDER OF RESPECT: CONCILIATION & EDUCATION, TORONTO, CANADA

In today's workspaces, relationships are just as important as results. That is exactly why Systems Inspired Leadership is an extremely valuable contribution, needed by so many right now! This book will provide leaders and team members with practical and implementable skills and meaningful questions they can integrate into their conversations immediately.

JENNIFER BRITTON, CEO OF POTENTIALS REALIZED, AUTHOR OF *RECONNECTING WORKSPACES* AND *FROM ONE TO MANY: BEST PRACTICES FOR TEAM AND GROUP COACHING*

What a timely and important book this is. It's insightful, relevant and offers very bite-sized and practical tools. I'm very excited that this material has now been shared with the world!

KATIE CHURCHMAN, SENIOR ASSOCIATE, 4D HUMAN BEING

Many leadership books speak to a time when businesses could create plans and implement them with relative ease. But Frank and Marita recognize that we now live in a world that demands a different style of leadership—one that leverages the collective intelligence of the system. This is a radical, vitally important leadership book that will help you develop the ability to lead from the system and successfully navigate complex challenges into an unknowable, emerging *future.* Systems Inspired Leadership *is the most advanced and important leadership guide for our times.*

GEORGINA WOUDSTRA, MCC, FOUNDER AND PRINCIPAL, TEAM COACHING STUDIO, CEO AND TOP TEAM COACH, AUTHOR AND SPEAKER

My mantra is 'achieve results by connecting people'. How to do that? In business society it is often about content. And that is logical. To create high performing teams is beyond only understanding content. It takes a lot more. It is also about talents, about behavior and about relationships. This book gives further insights about relationships, about the underlying patterns and systems. Have you thought about the patterns in your team, beyond the individuals? Do you play with that? Are you triggered? Read this book for inspiration and useful practices and tools to complete the journey with your team. This is part of leadership. Good luck in your journey.

GABRIELLE KALKWIJK, CEO ARDO

We all know that teams and relationships are more important than ever for business delivery. What makes this book special, is the fact that it offers a framework and practical ways on HOW TO understand and intervene in these systems in a completely different way. I know from my

own experience that the tools work and I am happy to see that it is now available broadly.

HAJNI SAGODI, OD CONSULTANT, ROYAL DUTCH SHELL

From my own experience, this framework is a breakthrough helping you realize your full potential and leverage the wisdom of all.

JOBBE JORNA, FOUNDER AND MANAGING PARTNER UPSTREAM CAPITAL

I believe that future organizations are fluid swarm-like eco-systems based on natural principles like resonance, flow, equality, and synergy. These new and highly agile organizations require a new kind of leadership—a type of leadership that is all about emotional intelligence, relationships, and creating an emotionally safe environment for all swarm members. This hands-on book pragmatically helps traditional leaders transform into leaders that thrive in these future organizations that consist of inspired and purpose-driven people. Our most significant challenge of changing to these kinds of swarm-like organizations is not about technology; it is about becoming more human.

CHRISTIAN KROMME, BESTSELLING AUTHOR AND GLOBAL FUTURIST KEYNOTE SPEAKER

What is it to be an ever more effective leader? Most good leaders I've worked with gave up "command and control" years ago. They have actively been studying Emotional and Social Intelligence, and yet, something is still missing. Here it is. Systems Inspired Leadership, *leveraging the principles of a 3rd Intelligence, namely Relationship Systems Intelligence, offers a theoretically sound, yet practical way to leverage the Intelligence of the System in a whole new way. In this book, Marita Fridjhon and Frank Uit de Weerd offer a step-by-step way for leaders and others to create more empowered and effective teams and relationship. This way of working is life-altering.*

**CYNTHIA LOY DARST, CPCC, ORSCC, MCC,
AUTHOR OF MEET YOUR INSIDE TEAM**

DEDICATION

To Faith Fuller, partner to Marita, thought leader, co-creator of the core curriculum and certification program in ORSC, and one of the most loyal, innovative, and loving beings on the planet.

To all faculty, partners, and alumni of the ORSC program, who were instrumental in the emergence of Systems Inspired Leadership.

CONTENTS

FOREWORD

I t is said that the only real constant in the world is change. And this has never been truer than it is today—with both the increased rate and intensity of change occurring for leaders, their teams, and their organizations. Factors such as sustainability, global competition, a changing/evolving corporate culture with diverse needs, a volatile political environment, and fast-paced technological advances are the major influences affecting these changes.

To benefit from these changes and flourish as an organization, both leaders and team members must evolve personally and develop group process skills to successfully leverage their diversity. In particular, they must possess the capacity to create an environment where dysfunctional conflict is reduced, and a healthy exchange of ideas and solutions can be explored to enable the organization to adapt and innovate.

Systems Inspired Leadership brings not only the theoretical concepts of such leadership, but also the practical tools and skills with which to navigate the complexity of our current world. Marita Fridjhon and Frank Uit de Weerd present a welcomed clarity and simplicity in their methodologies and field applications, making this book a must-read not only for leaders, but also for teams and nested systems in relationship with leaders.

At the very heart of their work is the message that "leadership is a role that belongs to the system." Going away are the old top-down, hierarchical ways of running an organization that simply no longer work in our modern world. Instead, *Systems Inspired Leadership* demonstrates that involving the system or team to co-author decisions and outcomes results in a highly agile organization where friction is significantly reduced, and new processes and products can evolve. In addition, with relationship strengthened at all levels, a sense of belonging is fostered—one of the biggest challenges facing corporate environments today.

The timing for the release of this book and the gems founds within couldn't be more appropriate. Any leader at any level, which pretty much includes all of us, who cares about evolving their organization as well as growing personally and professionally, would do well to read this book and apply its principles.

Doctors Arnold and Amy Mindell are avid researchers, global keynote speakers, and acknowledged by organizations ranging from UNESCO to multiple business and professional sectors for their leadership in cross-disciplinary work.

Dr. Arnold Mindell: founder of process-oriented psychology and author of twenty-three books in more than thirty-five languages, including *The Leader's 2nd Training: For Your Life and Our Work and Sitting in the Fire: Large Group Transformation Using Conflict and Diversity.*

Dr. Amy Mindell: process-oriented teacher, therapist, and author of *Metaskills: The Spiritual Art of Therapy.*

INTRODUCTION

If you are interested in a model of leadership that is better able to navigate the complexity and disruptive forces of the twenty-first century, this book is for you. This approach to leadership is less stressful and overwhelming and will help you leverage the intelligence and creativity of all. We call it Systems Inspired Leadership™ (SIL), an innovative approach to leadership that creates from the wisdom of the system without telling people what to do. It builds shared leadership at all levels of the organization. SIL is part of a growing trend towards more collaborative and collective leadership models.

The twentieth-century paradigm of heroic and individualistic ("the-leader-knows-all") leadership has become obsolete in a world that is increasingly complex and fast-changing. Still, many leaders and organizations work from this mindset, resulting in unhealthy pressure, anxiety, stress, and isolation.

Systems Inspired Leadership provides a powerful alternative. We have seen leaders become so much more impactful and fulfilled once they adopted a Systems Inspired approach and trusted what was trying to happen in a system.

Systems Inspired Leadership promotes a co-creative way of working that calls for a higher dialog quality than what normally occurs in organizations. It requires the ability to create psychological safety and ask challenging, disruptive, and catalytic questions. What's more, SIL encourages a willingness to listen, share hard truths, and allow the greater wisdom of the whole to come through in the process. One of the unique qualities of SIL is the recognition that, within any organization, there is an integrated system, and it too, has intelligence and a voice. Accessing that voice and wisdom will greatly help to navigate change, enhance agility, and propel innovation. And it will contribute to a deeper sense of meaning and belonging for the people involved.

Systems Inspired Leadership holds that leadership is a role of the system rather than of individual leaders and invites all employees and team members to step into their leadership. This requires leaders to perform their roles differently. In a way, they do less and focus more on revealing the system to itself in order to tap the collective wisdom and facilitate what is trying to happen. This makes the role of a leader not only more effective but also lighter and less stressful, as they realize that not everything rests on their shoulders.

If you are drawn to the above, this is the book for you. Our primary focus will be on the "doing" side of Systems Inspired Leadership.We will reveal the five key competencies for Systems Inspired Leadership and give you practical tools and tips on how to develop and deploy them. And, we consider personal or vertical development of Systems Inspired Leaders and teams as a given, as otherwise success might be hard to attain. We therefore have paid explicit attention to this in the latter part of the book. Ultimately, the book is about growing your Relationship Systems Intelligence™ (RSI), with a focus on its five principles. At the end of the book, you will find recommendations for implementing this approach within your team or organization. And throughout, you will find stories and quotes from interviews we conducted amongst practitioners to illustrate key points and help you fully understand and implement the key concepts of Systems Inspired Leadership.

HOW TO USE THIS BOOK

This book is meant to be a practical guide and field book, with some theoretical underpinning. We, therefore, invite you to explore it with a sense of adventure, visiting and revisiting the sections that grasp your attention and/or are most relevant to your current situation.

Chapters 1-4 provide the context, background, and origins of Systems Inspired Leadership and introduce the five key competencies. It is useful to start here.

Chapters 5-9 are the core of the book, dealing with the key competencies. This may be the area where you pick and choose, as a kind of manual. We have structured the material in such a way that you can go through it at your own pace. There is no fixed order to the competencies, so please feel free to select the ones you feel most aligned and comfortable with—or the ones that you find most challenging, depending on your learning style. Considering your team and its challenges, which competency might be most effective to bring into practice now? Make a commitment to yourself that this is not just an interesting read. Experiment with the ideas and practices in these chapters and find ways of prototyping them into your leadership life. This will not only help yourself evolving as a leader and human being, but also your team, the enterprise, and humanity.

Chapter 10 reviews the "being" side of Systems Inspired Leadership (this is about your personal or vertical development rather than your professional or horizontal development), and Chapter 11 discusses typical challenges that practitioners encounter when implementing Systems Inspired Leadership and ways to address these. In the Concluding Thoughts section, we will sketch some possible broader applications of Systems Inspired Leadership. They can all be read on their own.

At the end of the book, you will find for reference the glossary, the appendices, the literature list, and the acknowledgments.

If you wish to engage further with us or share your comments, please contact us through our websites or by email (for details, see section "About the Authors").

We wish you a great reading and leading experience!

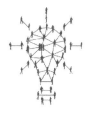

CHAPTER 1

EMERGENCE OF A NEW LEADERSHIP MODEL

"Rather than saying 'sort this out,' it is asking the team how can we go about this and listening to all the different voices."

- A CUSTOMER OPERATIONS MANAGER OF A MAJOR MULTINATIONAL

When we talk with leaders, we often hear stories about the accelerating speed of change and the resulting impact: pressure, stress, distrust, anxiety, and isolation. It gives the sense that you, as a leader, must carry it all alone—as if everything depends on you and so much is working against you. It is draining and often it feels there is hardly any recognition. As an example, let us listen to the story of a manager running an offshore customer service center in a big corporation.

"When I entered the office this morning, the first thing I saw was the email of my boss asking me how we do on customer first response time, so how quickly we respond to a customer request. I agree this is an important performance indicator, but it is not everything. I am aware that we do not do well on this indicator, but that is because we are understaffed. We have nine vacancies, you know, but we are not allowed to fill them because of cost pressure in the company. As a result, we put so much pressure on our people that some get sick.

I have now asked my staff to focus on 'first time right,' so closing a customer complaint in one go. This may take a bit longer, but I know this is more efficient in the long run. Unfortunately, some of our people do not get this. Ideally, I would like to replace them, but this is impossible given the company's policy of not filling vacancies.

So, rather than focusing on improving the operations and filling the gaps, I now need to spend time explaining to my boss what is behind the customer's first response time performance. He does not understand that looking at the past is taking away time to invest in getting my people to step up. And I have explained this to him already a million times, but he does not want to listen. Okay, I understand that he is probably being chased by his bosses, so he is passing the pressure on to me. He should not do that. He mentioned that there are probably some more cost-cuttings in the air. I really have no clue where these should come from. We are already cutting in our bones, and people are becoming more and more disengaged and getting sick. It is a vicious circle.

And of course, I understand that we need to step up our performance; I really do. Otherwise, there is a chance that they will close the customer service center. They have done it before, and I have seen other companies closing their centers here in the region already. We probably need to push our digital agenda, then we can do more with fewer people. It would be better if they helped me with that…

I am really not sure what it all means for me. It could well be that I must close the doors here, working like crazy to deliver a high-quality service till the end. And for what? Will they have another job for me? Will they still be interested in me, now that I am getting older? And if I lose my job, how will I provide for my family?

Sorry to be whining here—it helps me to release some steam. It brings me in a better frame of mind to answer the email of my boss. I will give him the explanation in a civilized and polite manner without rocking the boat. Let us keep the peace. Otherwise, I am sure I will pay the price."

What of yourself do you recognize in this person? What if you were able to:

- deal with pressure and being overwhelmed in a different way?

- build a strong collaboration with your staff and develop innovative solutions together?

- create strong employee engagement and deliver sustainable results?

- become more agile and create a high sense of belonging?

- feel confident and fulfilled because you are tapping into your best energy?

- feel connected and supported by the organization and part of a bigger whole?

- influence the wider organization effectively, tapping into what is wanting to happen?

- make your leadership more effective, fulfilling, lighter, and less stressful?

If you want more of the above, **Systems Inspired Leadership** is meant to help you. It is part of an emerging leadership approach that helps leaders deal more effectively with accelerated change and complexity in the digital age, the so-called VUCA world (volatile, uncertain, complex, and ambiguous). It moves away from the top-down leadership paradigm and promotes shared leadership at all levels of the organization. It invites you to create from the wisdom of the system rather than to react, and it reduces the feeling that everything depends on you. Instead of asking, "Who is doing what to whom?" the Systems Inspired Leader asks: "What is trying to happen?"

The New Global Business Environment

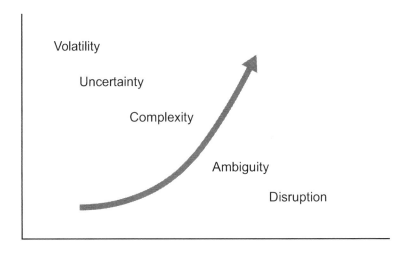

Systems Inspired Leadership is based on a **Relationship Systems Approach.** We know that the word "system" is sometimes confusing for people. In Chapter 3, we will discuss this more in-depth. For us, it is a shorthand for a group of interdependent entities working together around a common goal. A system can be a leadership team, a department (e.g., sales, manufacturing, finance), or an organization. It can also be two people working together. The key is that there are parts (e.g., individuals, departments, subsystems) with relationships between these parts. Systems Inspired Leadership's prime focus is on the relationships between the parts rather than on the parts themselves. Hence the *relationship* system qualifier. This approach works with the web of relationships, acknowledging that everything is interconnected and interdependent. Working with this web of relationships, and accessing the wisdom and intelligence that lives here, provides the key for a different way of leadership and working together. It is lifting the gaze from the individuals making up the system to the system or team itself.

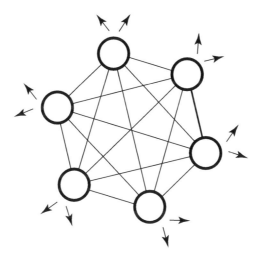

For example, a common approach to address performance issues is to focus on individuals, e.g., by sending them to training, providing them with coaching, or even firing them. This is often ineffective as the underlying system's dynamics will not be addressed. The issues often do not reside in the parts but the interdependence between them. The solution more often lies in focusing on building conscious and intentional relationships. This creates/strengthens the web of connection between team members, and surfaces insights on how to move forward together in a more effective way.

At the core of Systems Inspired Leadership is **Relationship Systems Intelligence (RSI).** It refers to the ability to reinterpret an individual's own experience (and that of others) as an expression of the system. The experience is both personal *and* belongs to the system. For example, you feel disappointed and unfairly treated when you did not get the assignment you were looking for. This is both a very personal experience and an expression of how this system is operating (and likely this experience is living in other parts of the system as well). RSI focuses on the relationship system itself (rather than on the individuals/elements in that system) and enables the ability to create from the wisdom of the system and helps it grow and evolve. Five important principles underpin RSI, which we will discuss in Chapter 3.

In the traditional command and control organizations of the past, IQ was seen as the key attribute of leadership. IQ remains important, of course, but in this VUCA world, more is needed for team and organizational efficacy. In the final decade of the last century, thanks to the work of Daniel Goleman in particular, it became clear that Emotional Intelligence (EQ) and Social Intelligence (SI) are important differentiators for great leadership.

- Emotional Intelligence is the ability to be aware of your own emotions and taking responsibility for actions flowing from those.

- Social Intelligence is the ability to accurately read the emotions of others and the capacity to empathize.

We hold that RSI is the next key differentiator for twenty-first-century leadership. It includes and transcends EQ and SI and takes intelligence to the realm of the relationship system, and what is available from and through that. The aim throughout this book is to help you grow your RSI and become more masterful at it.

The Growing Importance of RSI

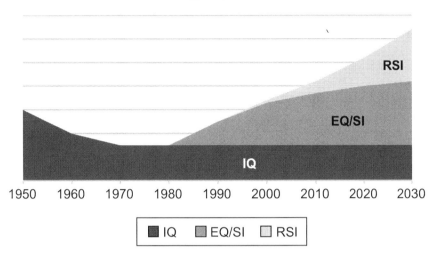

We have written this book for people who are keen to explore and adopt a different kind of leadership. One that is more people and systems inspired, that knows how to create from the wisdom of living relationship systems such as teams and organizations. This style makes maximum use of the intelligence and experience of its employees and of the wisdom of the relationship system itself. It can be for *leaders in hierarchical organizations* (profit, non-profit) who want to feel less imprisoned and create more freedom and flow. Equally, it supports *leaders in self-managed and swarm-like organizations* who actively distribute their leadership and work with the purpose of their organization. This book is also helpful for *professionals in the field of change*, like change agents and change managers, human resources professionals, organizational development specialists, (team and agile) coaches. And of course, also for *employees* who want to approach their organization in a different, more systems inspired way. We hold that leadership is not restricted to a job title in an organization. Even more so, we believe that leadership is a role of the system and if everyone steps into their leadership, a lot could change for the better.

Systems Inspired Leadership draws heavily on the teaching and practices of Organization and Relationship Systems Coaching™ (ORSC™). ORSC is the flagship program of CRR Global, a well-known international coach training school based in the USA, specializing in working with relationship systems such as teams and organizations. While the program's focus is on training coaches and consultants, an increasing number of people in leadership and agile roles are joining the curriculum. It shows the emerging interest and desire to apply the relationship systems approach to leadership in organizations. It is from this flagship program and its contribution to modern systems thinking, that Systems Inspired Leadership is evolving.

As part of the research for this book, we interviewed thirty people with not only extensive ORSC experience but also in leadership positions in different corporate sectors globally. The goal was to obtain empirical evidence on how this approach informed, influenced, and evolved their leadership. The interviewees cover four continents and twelve countries (Czech, Dubai, Germany, Israel, Japan, Mexico, Netherlands, Singapore, South Africa, Turkey, UK, USA; see next page) and represent a wide range of roles and companies (corporates, government agencies, consultancy, NGO, small and medium-sized enterprises). Throughout the book, we will use quotes from these interviews to illustrate key points and enhance the text.

Let us now return to the manager of the offshore customer service center whose story we heard at the start of this chapter. How would it be if this person was calling a gathering with her staff to discuss where they are and how they could improve their situation? Maybe they came up with some powerful ideas on how to deal with it. Maybe they set up mastermind groups to capture best practices, or visited other customer service centers to get inspiration and ideas. Maybe they invited an agile coach to help them to improve their processes. Maybe they called in an ergonomics expert to redesign the space to enhance effectiveness and well-being.

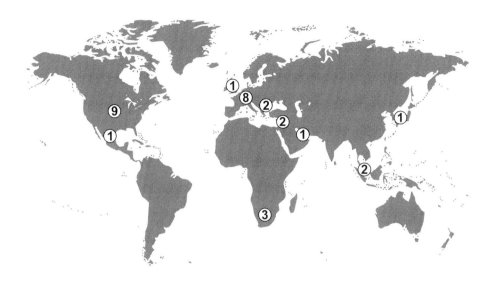

What if this person raised the topic of pressure in the team of her superior? Maybe they realized that this is a systemic issue that all of them were suffering from? Maybe this insight gave them the energy and courage to try out new ideas? Maybe they introduced check-ins at the start of each meeting to let off steam? Maybe they gave themselves permission to name it when too much pressure was put on them? Maybe they set up work-streams to identify short-term actions and develop disruptive options? So many things are possible.

In the end, it is about trusting that the answer is already in the system and only needs to come to the surface. It is about tapping the collective wisdom and leveraging the intelligence and creativity of all. The key question then is how to do that? The remainder of this book is precisely about that!

CHAPTER 2

WHAT IS SYSTEMS INSPIRED LEADERSHIP?

"I fundamentally believe that across any discipline, If people were trained in Systems Inspired Leadership, we would have higher productivity, higher job satisfaction, and more engagement in our workforce, no matter what the positional authority level is."

- AN ASSOCIATE DIRECTOR OF A HEALTH SERVICES AGENCY

To give you a sense of what Systems Inspired Leadership looks like in practice, please find below some of the stories we heard in the interviews that helped shape this book.

The first one is from a chief operating officer (COO) of a consumer tribunal, responsible for dealing with 30,000 cases per year with an organization of fifty people.

"When I got promoted into the COO role, I started to broaden my focus because I was suddenly responsible not only for the legal processes but literally for every single process and activity you can think of in the tribunal. It is almost a shift from silo thinking into collective thinking. And that coincided with my relationship systems training.

I met this relationship systems practitioner, and he told me that he is doing work that is very good for team cohesion and getting things to work effectively. He indicated that if I am interested in learning more, that I should attend the foundational training, which would take two days only. I am a numbers-driven person, so if it would mean that I could get people to be more productive, more effective, and more efficient, I thought, 'well only two days can't hurt.' I went to that fundamentals course but I was skeptical at this point, I must say. You know, people want to know within the first two minutes, 'What is in it for me and how much time should I spend on this?'

My natural inclination is to focus on the results and drive these, because results are what is measured. However, with some time, I started to realize that if you shift your focus and sort out the people, the results will follow. And this is what interests me. So, at that point, I started to make an active and conscious shift from being more task- and output-driven to being more people-driven.

Initially, I was just looking at the average turnaround of timelines, ensuring that people deliver seven hours and fifty-six minutes out of every eight hours they work. It sounds very blunt to say it like that, but if you are target-driven, you are not really interested in what is going on with the human beings delivering the results. They are a means to an end. In such an environment, people can easily feel, 'They don't care about me. I am just a number, an object that is easily replaceable.'

And when I shifted my focus to creating the right environment for human beings and being more people-driven, my attitude and language changed. It was now about explaining to people that everybody is important. You are an important part of this organization; there is no difference between large cogs and small cogs in this big wheel. We see you and your contribution as pivotal for reaching the ultimate result. So, people get motivated easier. They get more engaged. They get the same and even better results, yet the environment is pleasant, and people enjoy coming to work. And now that is one of the things that I tend to preach to people quite a bit: you spend such a lot of time at work, you might as well enjoy it!

It is driven by the notion in the relationship systems approach that you are a part of a whole. You are a part of the larger system and you matter; you are important; you are a voice that we want to hear.

In terms of results, we basically achieved all our targets, and, in many instances, we've overachieved them. We have also got six consecutive clean audits, which is a big thing in the public sector.

By becoming more people-driven, I think my own soft skills have improved quite a bit. I can see the impact on the results. And my own work has become less stressful.

For me, it has been quite a shift. The relationship systems journey assisted me in opening and accessing skills that I did not know were within me. I am actually much more a people person than I actually thought."

The second story is of a finance director of a healthcare services agency with 1600 employees and a budget of $900 million.

"One of my divisions sponsored five cohorts of people to train them in the relationship systems approach, to expose them to Systems Inspired Leadership, and give them tools to work better across systems. For example, we have used tools related to roles: role clarity and how staff show up and occupy a role. This gives people language that neutralizes their experience rather than personalizes it. Instead of feeling insecure that they do not know what they are doing, they can say, 'I am new to my role.' Instead of saying that someone is stepping on their toes and annoying them, they can say, 'I think we have some role confusion.'

I think it has made staff feel more secure; it has given them a language to neutralize situations that could otherwise become personal or make people grouchy. They have a new way of problem-solving that doesn't lead as much to the blame game.

Looking at my own development, in my twenties and thirties, I was more attuned to tasks and accomplishments. In my forties, I started looking more at the people I supervised and became more attuned to developing them. I was influenced by the very early Gallup book First, Break All the Rules, *which advised looking at each person and what they need to develop and treating them differently based on their needs. I enjoy supervision and generally hear that people enjoy the supervisory relationship with me.*

But the point, though, is that I did not bring the reflective intentionality to my work to the level that I have today, until I went through the relationship systems training. The way I was giving myself permission to stop and intentionally look at the system and listen to the system, wasn't part of my repertoire. It is probably because there is a focus on 'go go go, get things done.' Giving myself permission to stop and listen to the system was a huge breakthrough that I have only figured out by doing the relationship systems training.

In order to reflect and pause, I have to stop doing and sit and think about what I am experiencing and what is going on around me, to listen to what people have said and reflect on it, and think about it from a space where I am not working. And if I am with somebody else, then it is the same kind of thing. We stop working on our agenda, and we just sit and think about what has happened, what is being revealed, and try to stop ourselves from going to solutions too quickly and unpack what we might be experiencing and what might be happening. And then with the larger group or with the affected people, we can go and try to unpack it there. But a lot of it is involved with just stopping the machine for a minute, the machine of productivity. And I am not saying that this work is not productive, because it is, but there is a certain kind of stopping or pausing that feels different than, you know, task-based work.

The result has been a keener ability to address systems issues with staff and systems partners. Taking that time to address relational issues, identify a shared mission, has deepened my ability to keep that shared mission at the center of the work, particularly through difficulties and disagreements."

The third story is of a customer operations manager of a major multinational closing their customer service center of 250 people.

"I have been in leadership positions for many, many years. I have done many great things, and I have done some really stupid things, and I have seen my own leadership style evolve from a very autocratic style into a much more Systems Inspired Leadership style. I am super excited about that transition because it is less stressful for me and the people around me and it makes leading so much easier.

Businesses usually have a lot of change going on. There is the usual day-to-day pressure, and then things can go wrong, which adds pressure on top of everything else. And that pressure usually sits squarely on the shoulder of the leader, as they're held accountable. And then that pressure gets passed down into the organization, sometimes in a very un-elegant way. Everybody is just expecting results and pushing for results and we call this business focus.

My responsibility was to oversee the closure of a 250 people strong operation. Our biggest risk during this twelve-month closure journey was 'deterioration of service delivery.' Being Relationship Systems trained, I focused on the people around me and the energy in the room and began asking questions like, 'How do we want to do this? What is important for us? What is going to help us?' Just asking these questions and getting input moves away from the typical leader approach of: 'Guys, we need to sort this out! I want this, this, this! You need to get on top of that, we're going to do this, we're going to do that.'

The expectation that all the answers need to lie with the manager is an old myth and it is a trap that managers fall into. The myth is that I, as the manager, need to come up with the answers, and the quicker I come up with the answers, the better I am as a manager. It is a massive relief to realize that there are twenty or more other people from whom I can find out what they're thinking and feeling. What looked like a burden is actually a resource.

It made me realize that just focusing on getting it done doesn't necessarily speed up the process of getting it done. My reflection is that if we respect each other and remain connected to the emotional field, that the work gets done.

In the leadership team and in all the engagements, there was actually very little conversation about what we had to deliver from a project delivery point of view. Some of the leadership team meetings were too chaotic, some team members felt. And I said yes, there is a phase that will feel chaotic because we are in a chaotic state with all the change that is impacting people professionally and personally. These leaders were also impacted, and they needed to vent their emotions. They can't be chaotic and be venting on the operations floor, but we can create a space for that in the leadership team. So, we closed the doors and focused the first part of the meeting on how people were feeling. Just creating space for whatever needed to come up allowed things to settle again. And then everyone could focus on the work. Interestingly, there was no ball dropped from a business delivery point of view and the feedback from the organization was that the project was amazingly well delivered. I think this really happened as a result of the emotional connectivity that was available for everybody.

What is really difficult when we are under a lot of pressure is that our stress reflexes aren't wired up to say: 'Oh, let us tap into the emotional field of the system or let us get lots of voices in the room.' Most of our pressure reflexes say: 'Let us just get this done now and so the pressure gets pushed into the system from management and that has a tendency to break relationships rather than maintain them.' So, I think part of it is fighting against one's own stress reflexes.

We should not underestimate how much creativity, good ideas, and solutions sit in our organizations. What I see is that often as leaders we think that the next disruptive idea or solution comes from the outside or from management or consultants. But there are voices and views inside your system that could point to the next industry disruption that you might not be anticipating or that you could initiate as an organization. It requires that, as a leader, you really listen to the "2 percent truth" within those very disruptive and often complaining voices. As a leader, it can take, I know from my own experience, a lot of disarming of my natural reflexes to really listen to these voices especially when the message comes in a package that triggers me."

Three different people, three different stories, three different manifestations of Systems Inspired Leadership. What do they have in common?

The first element that stands out is *the focus on people* rather than on tasks. This is about seeing people first of all as human beings rather than as resources to get the job done. In systemic terms, human beings are also relationship systems in themselves. It is about valuing *the whole human being* and respecting *all* parts within self and the relationships between them. This focus on the whole person produces different and more sustainable results than by focusing on outcome and task only. For some people, this is counter-intuitive and feels like an unnecessary detour. In the interviews, we saw a number of people who were task-focused initially and became aware of the value of being more people-focused to achieve results. People are not replaceable objects, means to an end, pawns in a production game, or irritating obstacles in getting things done. This may have worked in the twentieth century, in a culture of assembly lines. But in a world with high complexity and accelerated change, this is not applicable anymore. It now becomes important to draw on the unique and creative qualities of people. This requires seeing people first as human beings, acknowledging their dreams, needs, strengths, and emotions. It highlights why Emotional and Social Intelligence are such important elements of Systems Inspired Leadership. As Antonio Damasio, a famous Portuguese American neuroscientist, states, "We are not thinking machines that feel, we are feeling machines that think."

A second element that comes through strongly in the above stories is *the focus on relationships, relationship systems, and Relationship Systems Intelligence*. This shift to the web of relationships is critical to address twenty-first-century challenges. Paul Polman, former CEO of Unilever, once said: *"The issues we face are so big and the targets are so challenging that we cannot do it alone… When you look at any issue, such as food or water scarcity, it is very clear that no individual institution, government, or company can provide the solution."* We are all part of a bigger whole; the whole is more than the sum of the parts, and every voice counts and has wisdom. It is ultimately about hearing from the system itself—not just the members—what is needed in what is currently emerging rather than staying stuck in old and broken patterns. It is shifting the focus from "who did what to whom" to "what is trying to happen." The ability to tune into the system becomes important, as well as the ability to pause and reflect, and the ability to listen to the different voices to tap the collective wisdom. There is also the notion that leadership is a role that belongs to the system rather than the person with the word "leader" in their job title, making leadership so much easier, lighter, and less stressful. In all stories, the importance of Relationship Systems Intelligence (RSI) is apparent. As indicated in the previous chapter, we hold RSI as the core of Systems Inspired Leadership and a key differentiator for twenty-first-century leadership.

The third common element in the above stories is how much the players *draw from the Organization and Relationship Systems Coaching (ORSC) approach.* They all were extensively trained in it. ORSC is a powerful coach training program that brings systemic interdependence and relationship systems to the foreground. It offers practical, tool-based approaches to working with relationship systems, combined with the opportunity for significant personal and transformational growth. You can find more information about ORSC and adjacent training with CRR Global in **Appendix 1.**

When we initiated the interviews, we were touched by everyone's willingness to contribute, without hesitation. It felt as though people were happy to do something in return for what they had received. In the interviews, a lot of gratitude was expressed about what the relationship systems approach has brought them, both personally and in their leadership. Below are comments from several people:

I remember going back to my boss after the first course and saying I've just taken the first step of the rest of my life.

I would have loved to have the relationship systems tools thirty years ago when I started.

I would say that regardless of what space you are in, this approach will meet you where you are. And all the tools work great.

It was like something that I knew in my body, but I've never thought about to verbalize.

Our family system has shifted tremendously, we are much more skillful in our relationships.

Imagine the impact people can get from this approach when exposed to it.

There's something in me that leans towards systems, loves the system work but this approach gave it meaning, gave it tools, gave it a language.

I was learning new techniques but it was also working on me as a human being. Led me to a greater level of maturity.

So, what is Systems Inspired Leadership (SIL)? It can be defined as *the ability to create and lead from the system, trusting that the answer is already there and waiting to be revealed.* Rather than directing the system, Systems Inspired Leaders facilitate emergence. They work with and rely on the system to give birth to what is trying to happen in that system. They hold leadership as a role of the system and grow shared leadership at all levels in the organization. It is a different way of leadership, both in terms of being and doing with Relationship Systems Intelligence (RSI) at the core.

In practical terms, it is the adoption of the relationship systems philosophy, principles, skills, and tools in the realm of leadership.

In the next chapters, we will discuss the core components (RSI, doing, being) in more detail.

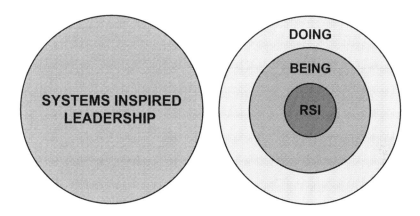

Let us also be clear that Systems Inspired Leadership is not about endless conversations, or deferring difficult decisions, or refraining from taking responsibility for choosing a direction. Someone or a team of people will need to make a decision, which may not be everyone's choice. Adopting a Systems Inspired Leadership approach, however, allows the team or system to be co-authoring the decision-making process in a very different way.

Systems Inspired Leadership aims to accomplish a shift in attention, without losing the benefits of the old approach. The aim is to include and transcend. It is manifesting a new leadership paradigm, shifting attention from the traditional to the new:

FROM	TO
Parts/Individuals	Relationship system itself/Web of relationships
Task/Process	People/Relationships
People as objects/resources	People as whole human beings, in relationship
Me	System of *We* and the system of the larger whole
Being in (the world of) thoughts	Being present to all channels of experience
Directing/Telling what to do	Revealing the system to itself
Analyzing	Sensing
Solving problems	Inspiring solutions
Known	Unknown/Emergence
Reacting to	Creating from
Speed of Change	Pace of evolution

Based on the interviews, we found five major impact areas for Systems Inspired Leadership:

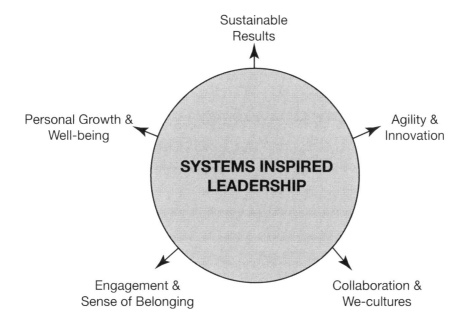

Here are some illustrative quotes from the interviews:

RESULTS	*"We are growing 8 percent this year, at a lower cost level, developing all kinds of new products, which we are launching in a shorter time."*
AGILITY	*"We realize that when we are leaning into the system, we are able to respond much faster and are much more current and relevant in delivering the results."*

INNOVATION	*"In our organization, we want to create something new/different, and really work with the system to create the emerging future."*
COLLABORATION	*"Really listening to the marginalized voices has shifted the partnership of our organizations and its ability to dream what is possible."*
WE-CULTURES	*"How do we want to deal with this? What are the problems that we are facing? What can we do to solve this?"*
ENGAGEMENT	*"People feel more proud to work in the department, and it is easier to attract talent."*
SENSE OF BELONGING	*"Just knowing that I'm part of this system and I belong to it. My words and my experience have a place. I can put it somewhere."*
PERSONAL GROWTH	*"It's just given me more depth and made me feel more confident and calm."*
PERSONAL WELL-BEING	*"As a leader, there is a huge amount of relief. You do not need to know it all, you can tap into the intelligence of many people. It's less stressful for me and everybody else."*

CHAPTER 3

RELATIONSHIP SYSTEMS AND RELATIONSHIP SYSTEMS INTELLIGENCE

"It is important to hold the systemic view, the view that someone is part of many interdependent systems."

-THE CEO OF A GLOBAL COACH TRAINING AND CONSULTING COMPANY

When we work with people, we notice that the term "system" is sometimes confusing. Some associate it with technology and information or management systems. Others have an anonymous dark entity in mind that is running your lives as a "Big Brother." And some associate it with family systems and constellations where emotional issues linked to early childhood are being addressed.

In this book and the paradigm it grew from, our focus is on the *relationship* system itself. In its simplest form, it can be defined *as a group of interdependent entities with a common focus or goal.* This can be an organization, a department, a leadership team, a project team, or a duo. A group of people as such is also a system. Consider people going to the cinema. Their common purpose is to watch the movie. If a fire alarm goes off and people need to go to the emergency exits, their interdependent nature will instantly come to the surface.

We are always part of multiple nested systems, in work, with families, friends, etc. And these systems are all interdependent. Something happening to one impacts all the others. A key challenge (and opportunity!) in systems thinking is how to remain aware of all the (nested) systems in action in any given situation. The number of relationship systems can be overwhelming and demarcation of who is in which system (or systems) is critical, while considering the complexity of overlapping systems as well.

A Systems Inspired Leader needs to have cognizance of this and be aware of which system is in the foreground at any time. One example is when we undertake a team assessment as part of a coaching intervention. The names of those who are part of the team often change as we engage with team members and regularly more people get added! We may think that we have clear boundaries in terms of who is involved, but it is not always that simple. Who are the key players in each department? What are the subsystems within that department? Who is overlapping with whom in which team? Who is on your leadership team? Who does my team interface with that significantly impacts what we are doing?

The systemic lens is, in fact, a Copernican Revolution. It is looking at the whole and the web of relationships rather than at the individual parts. This approach is not immediately intuitive for many. We are deeply imprinted to look at the parts or individual players, not at the complex web of connection between parts. How often have you heard about the bad apple on the team? Or the bad boss? Or the sick department? These are all indicators that people look at the parts rather than at the relationships between parts, whilst a systemic view would be more beneficial. Hence the old saying: "You can fire the employee, but you cannot fire the role." William Tate, a well-known scholar in the field of systems thinking, introduced the beautiful metaphor of the fish tank with sick fish. Our focus is normally on the fish, while the actual issue is the water in which the fish live. The narrow view of replacing the fish does not make sense as every fish eventually would fall ill. A more holistic approach is needed.

In this context, it is useful to distinguish between complicated and complex challenges (the Cynefin framework of Dave Snowden).

Examples of *complicated challenges* include how to build a driverless car, how to build a spaceship to transport people to Mars, or how to develop nanobots to attack cancer. It is basically a technical issue, a mathematical and physical puzzle where the right answers exist and where experts of many disciplines come together to co-develop the solution. The prime logic here is cause and effect thinking. There are technical solutions, and together we can find them.

Examples of *complex challenges* include how to create a high-performance culture in an organization, how to build more safety and trust in a team, or how to become more purpose-driven. This is not a technical issue where a set of experts can determine the correct intervention for the desired state. Here, cause and effect thinking falls short—there is not a technically right answer. In fact, technical solutions are often counterproductive. For example, in the case of creating a high-performance culture, an intervention could be to introduce a policy to dismiss the poorest performers. Maybe this strategy works, maybe not. This policy could create so much fear and individual focus that teamwork is compromised, and the overall performance of the company deteriorates. A common reaction in such a situation is to push harder—in this example to dismiss more people.

And the impact could be even more disastrous.

In complex challenges, the cause-and-effect relations are so complex that you can only determine afterward what precisely happened. And if you had this knowledge, it would not give you a recipe for a next similar challenge, as the actual conditions will not be the same. To go back to the original situation to try something else is impossible as the situation has changed (i.e., the milk is in the coffee now and you can't separate the two anymore). Here, cause and effect thinking has to be replaced by a systemic approach, which takes into consideration the interdependent nature of systems, where everything is related and interacts with each other.

We are so trained in cause and effect thinking that we apply this approach also to complex challenges and relationship systems. But the straightforward cause and effect approach does not suffice here. It requires a different approach and intelligence. That is why we put *Relationship Systems Intelligence* at the core of Systems Inspired Leadership. Developing this intelligence will help you to deal effectively with challenges in relationship systems and to identify interventions that can truly shift systems.

The key is to be clear on whether something should be viewed through the lens of the complicated or the complex, as this will determine the way to deal with it. Sometimes, there are aspects of both in an issue. Be aware of which one(s) you are navigating!

Complicated Challenges	Complex Challenges
• Technical/Mechanical issues (e.g., build driverless cars, develop nanobots that attack cancer, build stronger microchips) • Cause and Effect approach • Focus on the parts • Interdisciplinary team of experts to determine the right answer • IQ • Metaphor: "machine"	• Human/Relationship issues (e.g., build an agile organization, become more purpose driven, improve psychological safety) • Systems approach • Focus on the interconnections • Tapping the collective wisdom to determine the course of action • Relationship Systems Intelligence (RSI) • Metaphor: "living organism"

In this context, it is also useful to mention *"wicked problems."* These are social or cultural problems that are hard or impossible to solve, as there is no agreement between stakeholders about problem definition and possible solutions. Examples of wicked problems include how to deal with climate change or starvation. Often, solving one aspect of the problem will result in unintended consequences in other parts. For example, in the COVID-19 crisis, the social distancing needed to prevent the virus from spreading created more loneliness and depression. Addressing these problems requires dealing with cultural and behavioral patterns in a system. Intense stakeholder engagement, visualizing desired futures, and prototyping possible solutions are useful ways to deal with this. And all these approaches will benefit significantly from Relationship Systems Intelligence.

This brings us to the five *principles of Relationship Systems Intelligence*. These were first articulated in the article "Relationship Systems Intelligence. Transforming the Face of Leadership" (Fridjhon, Fuller, and Rød) and the book *Creating Intelligent Teams* (Rød and Fridjhon). Please note that whilst we are addressing them in a linear fashion, they are, in fact, interdependent and one cannot be seen as more important than the other.

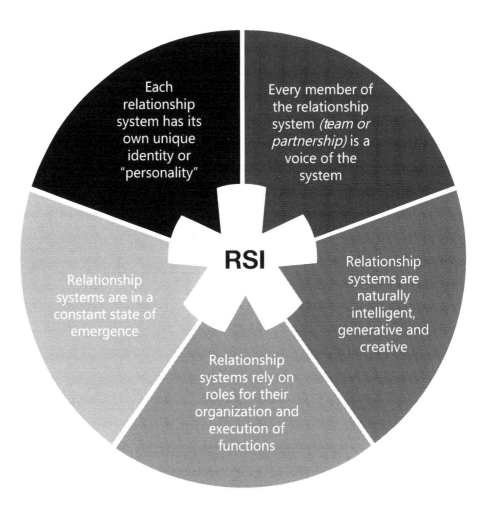

Let us look at each of them in detail.

Each relationship system has its own unique identity or "personality."

The moment people come together, an identity is created with its own unique set of qualities and characteristics. An example is the Beatles. The combination of the four individual members created an identity that was so much bigger than each of them, and together they created music that pleased millions of people and changed music history.

And look back at your own experience: no relationship is the same. You will notice that in each relationship system, some different aspects of yourself come to the surface. For example, in some you are more introverted, in others, you are more extroverted. It depends on the relationship system you are in, its purpose and outcomes, and the unique mix of people you are with.

We hold that each relationship system is a living organism, with its own identity, purpose, consciousness, strengths, desires, needs, wisdom, and potential. For many people, this is a new perspective. Our invitation is to start embracing this point of view and discover its power. It will shift your focus from yourself and others to the relationship system. In the relationship systems approach, we call this phenomenon the *3rd entity*. It is not me, it is not you, it is the 3rd entity: the relationship between you and me (or in the case of more people: the web of relationships between the members of the system). Like individuals, this 3rd entity has its own personality: an expression different from any system. We will explore this more in Chapter 5 with an exercise that will provide you with an experience of the 3rd entity.

Several people we interviewed indicated that this point of view, and particularly the notion of 3rd entity, was a breakthrough for them, something that they had not considered before and that impacted their leadership significantly.

"The 3rd entity is the missing link. I thought—ooh that is also a way to look at it. I knew I missed something and that I was focused too much on individuals and this was the answer."

- A CORPS STAFF OF A POLICE DEPARTMENT

Every member of a relationship system (team or partnership) is a "voice of the system."

Each voice is both deeply personal *and* an expression of the whole relationship system. The system itself is limited in how it can communicate; it relies on its individual members to express itself. We often think that what happens to us and what we experience is completely unique to us. This is true, of course, from one perspective, as we have our own unique personal history, experience, and personality. On the other hand, it also may be a systemic issue or event expressed through you. Other people may experience something similar. For example, you were disappointed with your performance appraisal and started doubting yourself. It is very likely that others have comparable experiences. The deeper explanation could be that your performance appraisal system does not allow for many top performers and disappoints many as a result. This principle puts your experience in a broader perspective, depersonalizing it, and, therefore, it may help you to take things less personally and get to acceptance quicker. It allows you, as a leader, as well as the team, to investigate whether and how this might be a voice of the system that is expressed through you.

A customer operations manager shared in the interviews that he used this principle very consciously when he felt a lot of anxiety: *"Oh, I am probably not the only one with this in the system. If it is in me, it is also in the bigger team/organization. Ok let me find out."*

You can also see this principle in action if you want to say something (e.g., "We are circling around this topic") and someone else voices it at the same time. Apparently, it was "in the air" and someone needed to say it. One of our interviewees took this even broader and said: *"If I had more systems skills at a younger age, I would have suffered less; I would not have taken things so personally."*

As a Systems Inspired Leader, it is important to invite input, allow every voice to be heard, and hold it as having value. This may require courage as people may have to voice things that are difficult (e.g., "I think we don't listen well to each other right now"). However, it is important for the health and success of the system that this information comes to the surface. And what you say is not necessarily always your very personal view. It is just a voice of the system that needs to be spoken and you can choose to serve as the instrument. What it builds over time is a sense of safety and trust within a team, also if not every voice or opinion is executed upon.

Another implication of this principle is that every voice counts and has wisdom. Every voice contains relevant information to consider, including the marginalized voices or the voices that you don't like so much. The resistors, the complainers, the jokers, the risk avoiders—all have some part of the truth. It links to the notion of Deep Democracy, a term coined by Arnold Mindell, which holds that every voice has wisdom.

This point can be illustrated by the famous Indian story of the blind men examining an elephant. According to one, it is like a trunk; for another, it is like a leather blanket. Someone else claims it is like a snake, and for yet another, it is like a brush. And all are right from their perspective. It is only by combining all the information that the full picture emerges.

A CEO phrased it as follows in our interviews: *"For me, leading systemically means championing no one is wrong, no one gets to be wrong, but we get curious, and everybody plays a very important role in the team, no matter where they are in the hierarchy."*

And the technical services manager said: *"When someone says something, I learned that they're not speaking on behalf of themselves but of the system."*

Relationship systems are naturally intelligent, generative, and creative

This principle is in our professional training often received with some disbelief. Systems are often associated with rigidity and the tendency for the status quo. While historically this bears some truth, modern systems thinking brings a different positivity to the table in trusting that once the system is revealed to itself, the members of the system can tap the collective wisdom and trust that a course of action will become apparent that helps the system grow, evolve, and flourish. Equally, the trust and belief in the intelligence of the system allows people to engage with each other differently and opens the space for everyone's voice to express itself, including making space to hear the voice of the system.

It also holds that it is not a problem when the system is being challenged and it is not immediately clear what is going on or where to go next. The ability to sit together with uncertainty and not knowing is a really important element of Systems Inspired Leadership, as this phase precedes insight. Knowing that the system is intelligent, generative, and creative gives people the confidence and strength to "sit in the fire" and wait for insight to emerge. This is very different than the knee-jerk panic reactions that often happen when a system is under pressure.

The mindset here is to "see disturbance as an ally" (e.g., losing an important customer). How could this help us and be a trigger for innovation and development? What is the deeper learning here? What is the opportunity? Let us not waste the crisis!

Quotes from the interviews to illustrate this principle

"Just trusting that the system knows. This is what is happening right now and it is important."

- A CUSTOMER OPERATIONS MANAGER
OF A MAJOR MULTINATIONAL

"There is something about the system itself that has its own answers. That frees up the individual and the leader from the pressure to come up with the answer."

- THE CEO OF A GLOBAL COACH TRAINING
AND CONSULTING COMPANY

Relationship systems rely on roles for their organization and execution of functions. Roles belong to the system, not to the individuals that inhabit the system.

We consider a relationship system to be a living organism with its own needs. These needs can be fulfilled by roles taken up by the individuals in the systems. These can be *outer roles,* covering the jobs and tasks required to keep things running smoothly, like CEO, head of marketing, or VP operations. And *inner roles* for the emotional functioning of the relationship system, like initiator, pursuer, visionary, disturber, and finisher.

It is a powerful idea to state that these roles belong to the system. So often, people identify themselves with an outer role ("Mr. or Mrs. Sales"), forgetting that they are both more and less than the role. In the space of outer roles, we often see role confusion (e.g., "what is in and what is out?) and poorly occupied roles (e.g., a logistical service that does not exist yet).

The emotional maintenance of a system normally requires a wide range of roles, covering polarities like seriousness/lightness, initiating/finishing, and challenging/appeasing. We notice a lot in our practice that inner roles are occupied unconsciously, often based on someone's natural strengths or preferences. For some people, it is easier to challenge, and others are better at creating harmonic relationships. Some people are more serious by nature, and others bring more lightness. If these roles are distributed unconsciously, this can create different camps in the system causing unhealthy dynamics. And there can be "role nausea," the feeling that you always have to take responsibility for the same thing, and you are fatigued by it (e.g., asking the challenging or catalytic questions which are often seen as taking the role of disturber).

It is, therefore, important for members in the system to regularly review and discuss role occupation and functioning, both for outer and inner roles.

An important implication of this principle is that leadership is also a role of the system. It does not belong to one person (even if the job title suggests they are the leader). We hold that leadership can and should be assumed by all members of the system, in a very organic way—as a dance of leading and following. We have learned that it is important to educate members of systems about this. For some, this idea is very scary while for others, it is liberating.

One example of this was in a workshop that Marita was part of in a Retreat Center in Switzerland. Participants were participating in a Deep Democracy process facilitated by Arnold Mindell and colleagues. Things got heated, and at some point, it became rather chaotic with everybody being loud and feeling agitated. Facilitators worked hard to create empathy and understanding while the loudness continued. At that point, a small girl with Down Syndrome wandered into the room. She started going up to individuals in distress, touching them gently saying, "Shhh, it's ok, don't be upset..." Within minutes, a room of 250 professional adults got quiet and settled down. In *that* moment, the role of leadership was powerfully occupied by a small child who might be seen as somebody with a disability.

Quotes from the interviews to illustrate this principle

"Roles, internal roles, external roles, the fact that they belong to the system means that we can populate them differently."

- THE CEO OF REGIONAL COACHING AND
TRAINING ORGANIZATION

"A new [business] development could mean laying off people. This then is based on what roles are needed and being occupied in the system. It is about roles, not about bad people."

- THE SENIOR AGILE PROGRAM MANAGER
OF A GLOBAL CONSULTANCY

Relationship systems are in a constant state of emergence, always in the process of expressing their potential.

Change is always there. Nothing remains the same; there is always something that wants to happen, like the river that is never the same. Emergence is the way to deal with complex challenges and changes in relationship systems. It is more about sensing and acting on what is trying to happen rather than applying standard problem-solving techniques to identify the next interventions. Otto Scharmer, an important scholar in the field of systems thinking, calls this: "Leading from the emerging future."

A good example of emergence is the death of Johan Cruijff, the legendary Dutch soccer player, who passed away on March 24, 2016. After the news broke, what emerged was that people gathered spontaneously at the iconic places of his career to mourn the momentous loss: the parental home in Amsterdam and the stadiums of the clubs he played for (Ajax and FC Barcelona). There was also enormous coverage on TV, social media, and newspapers. Everyone in the Netherlands knows where they were when they heard the news. In Amsterdam, a walk was organized a couple of days later to express their appreciation and loss. Clubs stopped the game for a minute of silence in the fourteenth minute, referring to his shirt number 14. His death also triggered conversations about renaming stadiums to remember him. And now there are soccer stadiums in Amsterdam and Barcelona carrying his name.

Where did this all come from? No one organized the spontaneous gatherings on the day of his death. They simply happened as a systemic expression of what was wanting to happen. It was somehow in the air; it was an emergence in action.

If you start looking at this kind of phenomenon, you will see it more and more in action. We as human beings are not yet skilled in dealing with this. Or, perhaps, we have not yet given ourselves permission to practice this ability or felt safe enough to experiment with it. Sensing and knowing what wants to emerge, tapping into the collective wisdom, and creating from the system are very different and new ways to engage with the challenge. Relationship Systems Intelligence builds this capacity. And it is not that everything happens spontaneously. For example, renaming the Ajax stadium to Johan Cruijff ArenA took more than two years, in view of legal and commercial considerations. But the idea and direction were born when he passed away.

This principle addresses the root of what the main conversation is now around the speed of change. With this principle, we can normalize change as a natural event. When we can do that, we can change the rhetoric to the powerful question: what is trying to happen here? What can we create from this? It immediately shifts the stance from reacting to creating from what is emerging and knowing that everything is a prototype. The real challenge is that we often do not pay attention to the emerging signals of change and wait until it is too late. That is when it becomes an emergency!

This is something we saw, for example, with the outbreak of the COVID-19 crisis in 2020. Some countries and organizations were much better at sensing what was happening, taking a pause, reflecting on what is trying to happen, and only then determining their course of action. And it is not so much that they knew immediately the right course of action (you never know in a complex world), but they were willing and able to see what was there and then determine their response, building on their learnings and insights. This is quite different from ignoring or blaming the virus and reacting without taking a pause and proper reflection—or to start panic-buying. CRR Global (the organization delivering relationship systems training worldwide), for example, used the outbreak to start offering virtual courses. These had already been considered and, now it was the time to put them into the world.

Emergence happens when a system becomes aware of itself. Once it can see itself, it can rearrange itself and to self-correct where needed. As we will see in Chapter 7, a Systems Inspired Leader will, therefore, pay a lot of attention to revealing the system to itself, as this will make the system self-aware (e.g., when a team is avoiding making a tough decision). Revealing this will create awareness and allow a shift. Technically, you could say that the parts constellate differently, such that new properties of the system emerge. It draws on the self-regulating nature of systems.

The art of Systems Inspired Leadership is to deal skillfully with emergence, pausing, and distilling what is wanting to happen, then to prototype that, discover how the system reacts, and then take it from there. It is very much a step-by-step approach, a learning journey where each next step requires reflection and relationship systems intelligence. It is very different from the classical change management approach using linear planning (the so-called "roadmap") to go from A to B. It is also very different from traditional problem solving (as applicable to the realm of complicated problems) where people optimize their part of the system and, thereby, often unintentionally, sub-optimize the whole.

Emergence is not always about radical change. It can also be a gradual emerging approach of seemingly minor changes, building on where the energy goes. But these seemingly small steps may add up to something significant, like a two- or three-degree tiller change in the course of a sailboat on a trans-Atlantic crossing. That small tiller change might not be perceptible in the moment. However, over time, it might land that boat at a different destination! For example, the appointment of a new leader or leader team creates ripple effects that go far beyond their unit, impacting the larger organization and beyond, creating whole new realities that a linear approach could never have imagined. The arrival of the internet, smartphones, climate change, and the pandemic are other examples of emergence leading to quantum change. Equally, Systems Inspired Leadership can be seen as part of an emergent wave of a more collective and collaborative leadership needed to address the complexities of the twenty-first century. Current developments in nanotechnology, genetics, AI, and robotics are creating the next waves of emergent and exponential change, impacting all areas of personal life, organization, and society.

An important indicator for emergence is disagreement and conflict. We hold that conflict is the engine of change. It is not problematic if there are different points of view in a system. On the contrary, it is simply a signal that change is needed, that something new wants to be borne. The more diverse the team is, the more different perspectives there will be, and the higher the potential of tapping the collective wisdom. At the same time, it provides a challenge to be able to listen and consider all voices and create constructive conflict to determine which course to take. In Chapter 8, we will come back to this in more depth.

Quotes from the interviews to illustrate this principle

"If we keep on bumping against the same obstacle, it is time for the question: what is trying to happen here?"

- THE CEO OF A GLOBAL COACH TRAINING
AND CONSULTING COMPANY

"In heavy conflict, I do resort to what is wanting to happen here now. The more I get better at this, the faster things happen."

- THE OWNER OF A REGIONAL EXECUTIVE
AND TEAM COACHING COMPANY

Lastly: The Systems Inspired Rule

Derived from the principle: "Every member of a Relationship System is a Voice of the System," we hold an important systems inspired rule: everybody is right… partially. When we introduce this in our relationship systems courses, many people start laughing. But after some time, the depth of this rule starts sinking in. It means that you are open to influence; you are willing to refrain from judgment, and you ask questions for which you truly have no answers. More importantly, you are interested in the marginalized voices since they may contain the seed of the new. It helps to make systems that are stuck more fluid, create more agility, and gain new information about what is trying to happen. It also helps to enhance safety and belonging, which is such an important foundation for dealing successfully with complexity and emergence. Adopting this rule requires personal maturity.

The Systems Inspired Rule:

everybody is right... partially.

CHAPTER 4

THE DOING SIDE OF SYSTEMS INSPIRED LEADERSHIP: THE S-CI-R-E-S MODEL

"The ones with a growth mindset say: 'I want to be a better leader, show me ways of doing that. Yet, show it to me in ways that are simple so that I can apply it.'"

- THE DIRECTOR OF TALENT MANAGEMENT OF A MAJOR MULTINATIONAL

During the interviews, it became clear that each leadership journey was very personal and unique and impacted by many influences and experiences. From that perspective, it was not possible to identify a particular style or profile. At the same time, it came through loud and clear that the relationship systems approach had played a significant role in the leadership of each of them, both in terms of "doing" and "being."

When reviewing the data, we discovered that Systems Inspired Leaders exhibit five competencies that enable them to create from the system and tap the collective wisdom. These competencies can be summarized by the acronym: S-CI-R-E-S™.

The S-CI-R-E-S Model

Working with
Conflict to
Facilitate
Emergence

Seeing,
Hearing and
Sensing the
System

Holding
Conscious and
Intentional
Relationship

Revealing
the System
to Itself

Creating
Systems
Inspired **S**afety

S =	Seeing, Hearing, and Sensing the **System**
CI =	Holding **Conscious** and **Intentional** Relationship
R =	**Revealing** the System to Itself
E =	Working with Conflict to Facilitate **Emergence**
S =	Co-creating Systems Inspired **Safety**

These competencies are not distinct. They are interdependent, they need each other, and they interact. To facilitate an in-depth understanding of each of them, we will deal with them separately. In the upcoming chapters 5-9, each competency will be reviewed. Every chapter starts with a **definition** and makes the link with the principles of Relationship Systems Intelligence. Then we will offer you powerful **ways of growing this competency**, highlighting **useful models, tools, and skills** to accelerate your learning. Each chapter ends with a **self-assessment**, so you can see where you are on a particular competency.

We invite you to educate, leverage, and train yourself and others in these competencies, step by step. There is no fixed order to them, so please feel free to select the ones you want to work on most. When you feel you have made sufficient progress, then switch to another aspect or competency and grow and integrate it. In this way, you will create an upward spiral and grow yourself into an ever more competent Systems Inspired Leader.

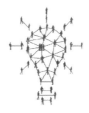

CHAPTER 5

DOING – SEEING, HEARING, AND SENSING THE SYSTEM

"I see systems as if they are real physical things. I didn't have that before. I now get the essence of that system."

- A DIRECTOR OF A HEALTH SERVICES AGENCY

Definition of "Seeing, Hearing, and Sensing the System"

- Ability to focus on the system as a whole and apply the principles of Relationship Systems Intelligence (RSI).

- Ability to "see" the systemic whole or constellation, "hear" the system by holding every voice as an expression of the system and by creating opportunity for collective input, and "sense" what is happening in the culture and atmosphere of the relationship system at any given moment.

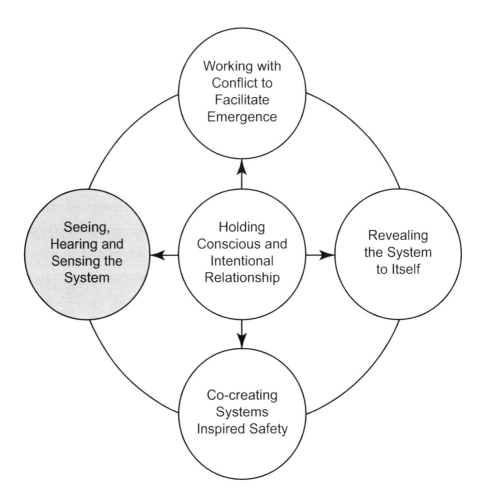

Link with Relationship Systems Intelligence (RSI)

While acknowledging that the RSI principles are interdependent and interconnected, the following principles link particularly well with this competency:

- Each relationship system has its own unique identity or "personality."

- Every member of a Relationship System is a "voice of the system."

Ways to grow this competency

In this chapter, we discuss six powerful ways to help you advance this competency:

> 1. Shift the focus from the individual parts to the systemic whole.
>
> 2. Engage with the relationship system as a living organism with its own identity and wisdom.
>
> 3. "See" the system: look for systemic constellations and metaphors.
>
> 4. "Hear" the system: hold every voice as a voice of the system.
>
> 5. "Sense" the system: track and work with the Energy/Emotional Field.
>
> 6. Educate your team/organization on Relationship Systems Intelligence and Systems Inspired Leadership.

1. Shift the focus from the individual parts to the systemic whole

Challenges in relationship systems usually reside in the connections between the parts rather than in the individual parts themselves. Systems Inspired Leaders, therefore, focus their attention on the systemic whole and the web of relationships and hold that as the entity for execution, innovation, and efficacy.

This is often counterintuitive as we are so used to the analytical approach of problem-solving that focuses on the individual elements. For example, in an effort to reduce costs, an organization may decide to reduce working capital by minimizing stock levels. The unintended consequence might be that customers get disappointed as their favorite product is out of stock. This will negatively impact customer satisfaction, which is another important performance measure. So, by optimizing one part of the organization, it may unintentionally sub-optimize other parts. It is, therefore, beneficial to shift the focus to the systemic whole and ensure coherence between the parts.

A story to illustrate the importance of focusing on the systemic whole is when Alan Mulally joined Ford Motor Company as CEO in 2006 when the company made a loss of $17 billion. He managed to turn the company around by creating trust, transparency, and collaboration between the departments. Classic is the story about a leader in one of Alan's first business review meetings who admitted that he had a production problem. Everyone thought that Mulally would dismiss him as this used to be the culture if you failed. Instead, Alan started to clap his hands and asked, "Is there anything we can do to help you?" And immediately his colleagues offered him ideas and resources, something that had not happened before.

Mulally was able to restore the relationships between the parts, reinstated the information flow, and improved the flow in the relationship system. Interestingly, Alan turned the company around with basically the same leadership team that almost led Ford to bankruptcy. The answer was clearly not in the individual parts but in the relationships between them. The outcome, in essence, was systems inspired rather than attained by any one individual.

Practical application

As a general rule, consider errors/failures/mistakes first as systemic events. For example, if someone is performing poorly, ask yourself:

- How is this an expression of the system?

- Where else is this happening in the system?

- What could be the systemic reasons for this?

- What about our team/organization is contributing to this failure?

Quotes from the interviews

"I started to observe the system more, looking for patterns, before I made it a one-to-one thing."

- THE CEO OF A GLOBAL TRAINING ORGANIZATION

"It shifts the DNA. It's fundamentally acknowledging the whole picture and how everything interconnects. It is conceptual at first, but when applied it becomes very realistic."

- A CUSTOMER OPERATIONS MANAGER
OF A MAJOR MULTINATIONAL

2. Engage with the relationship system as a living organism with its own identity and wisdom

Modern systems thinking is a considerable body of work focusing on systemic processes and evolution. It has brought creative ways to observe and work with systems and bring systemic understanding. Systems Inspired Leadership builds on this *and* complements it by bringing a strong focus to the relationship system as an entity, with its own "personality" and unique qualities and as holding information above and beyond the individuals populating the system. In Chapter 3, when we described the principles of RSI, we referred to this phenomenon as the **"3rd entity."** Empirical data from practitioners and case studies globally show us, again and again, that when this 3rd entity—that web of interconnection present in every set of relationships—is accessed, it often speaks from the meta-view and offers clearer information of what is trying to happen than can ever be obtained from the individuals populating the system.

The 3rd entity is the unique identity of a relationship system, separate and different from that of the players within it. In "day-to-day" language, people refer to it as "this team," "this duo," "this department," "this orga-nization," "this shop." It highlights the unique qualities, personality, char-acter, spirit, culture, and consciousness of that relationship system. It is the relationship system as a living organism, as a creature that breaths, sees, feels, moves, and makes sounds.

There are as many 3rd entities as there are relationship systems. This can be the relationship between two persons, but also the web of relation-ships in a team, an organization, or a country.

Please note that the system can only express itself through the thoughts, actions, movements, expressions, and diversity of its members. For this reason, Systems Inspired Leaders continue to value the contribution of each team member as an expression of the system. *And* they rely on the team to then lift the gaze beyond these individual contributions, to see, hear, and sense what the system will now know and wants to express from that new awareness.

We equally hold that this book was written by the 3rd entity of the two authors, rather than by the individual authors themselves. It is the combina-tion of the two of us that created this book. No other combination would have produced the same output and followed the same journey. And at times during our process, we too needed to consult our 3rd entity to deter-mine the best way forward, pondering the question: "What would the book want?" This was critical in creating the "one voice" of two very different and strong personalities when we did not always agree or see the same expression or outcome! When in doubt, we asked the book itself, which ultimately needed us to express what is important. And if you think about it, this book was, in a way, also co-authored by the people we interviewed, by the colleagues we spoke with during the writing process, by what we read in books and heard in conversations, by our conversations with the publisher, and by coincidental encounters that triggered new thoughts and insights. We might even imagine that an ever-expanding set of 3rd entities was engaged in co-creating this book.

The concept of "3rd entity" can be experienced in a variety of ways. It is derived from one of the first exercises in our Organization and Relationship Systems training program in which you explore a challenge in a valued and important relationship. First explore from your own position (the 1st entity), then from the other person's experience (the 2nd entity), and finally from the position of the relationship itself (the 3rd entity), reflecting respectively Emotional Intelligence, Social Intelligence and Relationship Systems Intelligence (see also Chapter 1). In the 3rd position, it is key to feel into it: what does it experience? What does it need? What does it know that the other two have forgotten about? It is not just a helicopter or detached view.

What is surprising for many people is that standing in the 3rd entity position actually provides them with new and powerful information. It enables you to look differently at the issue at hand and the actions you take. You access the voice of the system directly and tap into its wisdom. We encourage you to try this and experience it yourself. Get a sense of what we are talking about and allow yourself to start appreciating its power. In our experience, the 3rd entity often speaks the voice of wisdom and provides a less emotional perspective. The focus shifts from the short-term to the long-term, from a single stakeholder perspective to what benefits the whole. It helps you to experience the system from the balcony, in addition to the experience on the dancefloor.

When you participate in our training, you will see that we deliver them mostly with two trainers. We are co-leading, and participants often wonder how we do this as it looks so smooth, as if we talk with one voice. They ask us whether we have a script. The answer is no. We create from our own 3rd entity. It is not about who says what when; it is about leaning into our relationship and leading from our 3rd entity. We hold that our relationship is giving the course, not each of us separately. This requires significant preparation, a strong alignment on the key learning points, how we want to be together, a willingness to "dance" with decisions taken by your co-lead in the moment, and leaving behind your ego. And of course, this 3rd entity is also creating from the group in front of us by "seeing, hearing, and sensing" what is emerging from them.

The same is happening in high-performing teams. Players work together as a whole, doing what is needed in the moment to serve the team purpose, dancing flexibly together, acting as a flock of birds. Think of great sports teams, where players move dynamically to best position themselves for the team's success. Unfortunately, we also see a lot of individualism, silos, and fiefdoms in organizations. These so-called I-cultures are detrimental to the overall team and organization performance. Creating 3rd entity awareness is beneficial here. It helps to create we-cultures, cultures where achieving the common goal is more important than the success of an individual or organizational unit.

In the interviews, we heard a powerful example of how an organization used the 3rd entity exercise to determine how to cut costs during the financial crisis. They spent the whole day exploring this question from individual and departmental perspectives and documented possible scenarios. Towards the end of the session, they randomly divided the teams into small groups. The instruction was to feel into the system/entity of the organization itself; what does "IT" need? What does "IT" want them to do? When the groups returned and gave their report, to everybody's surprise, it became clear that there was overall agreement that certain functions that were outsourced should be brought in-house. Management and team members accepted this—including two team members directly impacted. It is very different when a decision like this is authored through collective input and from the organizational entity itself, rather than as a top-down decision from the leaders. It leverages the available information in the system and creates a greater sense of ownership and buy-in.

Marita accounts for another example: "*We were working for about a year with a global company working in the alcohol and gaming industry in process with a merger and acquisition. In this industry, there is a wide variety of clients and professionals involved: software engineers, legal experts, police, just to name a few. In the final session, there were 250-300 people in the room sitting at tables of ten. At the left of me, there was a group of police officers and a couple of lawyers. And one of the police officers was a gentleman that, while we had a good relationship, consistently played the needed role of 'disturber' for the system.*

Towards the closing of our session, we had a version of the 3rd entity exercise. We wanted them to look at all information gathered over the past nine months, but now from a very different place. We asked them to scan the information again, to take it in, and then to let it be. Then we gave them five minutes in silence to occupy the position of the merger. Imagine that you sit in the place of the merger. What does 'IT' want? What does 'IT' need from all of you sitting here in the room? What is its best hope? What is the challenge? What is the acknowledgment that 'IT' wants to give to you? The merger itself has a voice as well.

After the five minutes in silence, they had ten minutes to make some notes and have a table discussion. Then we brought them back to share their discoveries. The very first hand that was up was that of my police officer friend. For a moment, I just said internally to myself: 'Oh my goodness, what now?' But then he stood up and spoke. He had everybody's attention. What he said was, 'This activity, although I rolled my eyes before we started it, this conversation that I could have with the entity/system that is the merger has given me more information in five minutes than I have gotten over the nine months that we have been working together.' It was a decisive turnaround point in their journey of becoming one organization."

Practical application: 3rd entity exercise using team chair

- When discussing a particular decision, give each team member a chance to speak their viewpoint without interruption. You might even use a timer and give everybody one or two minutes and do several rounds to really flesh out input and relevant suggestions.

- Place a chair out in front of the team. Invite team members to step to the chair, and once in it, feel into what the system of the team or the team entity wants from them. What does "IT" know that individual team members might not know or have forgotten? What does "IT" need to move forward? Remind them that once in that chair, they are not speaking from their personal space. They are the voice of their system. They speak in first-person as "IT."

- Playfully call them out if you hear them speak from their own position, request they go back to their own seat, and take their own side again. Then when ready, move them back to the voice of the team system sitting in the chair.

- Empirical evidence and experiences with teams and organizations globally have proven repeatedly that there is a different set of information available when we can directly access the voice of the team, or the organization, or even the challenge. It is more neutral and usually provides new insight and awareness.

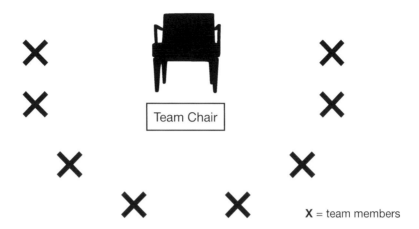

X = team members

Quotes from the interviews

"Before my relationship systems training, I wasn't focused on the system. I wasn't focused on the 3rd entity as something created by the group. I was aware of group dynamics but not of a 3rd entity."

- THE FINANCE DIRECTOR OF A HEALTH SERVICES AGENCY

"I believe that culture is a lot more important than strategy. If the 3rd entity is right, success will follow automatically."

- THE CEO OF A GLOBAL TRAINING ORGANIZATION

3. "See" the system: look for systemic constellations and metaphors

Constellations are a natural and easy way to "see" systems. It is like looking at a sky full of stars in the middle of a clear night. You see how they are positioned relative to each other; you notice the differences in brightness, and you start discovering patterns. To look at systems in this way, as the web of relationships, is very powerful and can unlock vital, often unconscious information.

Constellations appear in many shapes. For example:

- Look at where people habitually sit in meetings. Who is often sitting together? Who sits closest to the boss? Who is having the coffee conversations during the break? These are often unconscious manifestations of relationship patterns. If your team has a fixed seating arrangement, consider shuffling this and enquire about the impact.

- Network analysis can also highlight relationship systems. Who has a rich network? Who is a hub, connecting different sub-systems (or nested systems as they are also called)? Who has strong relationships with the top of the organization or with the external world?

- Virtual meetings have given rise to interesting constellations as well: Who has the video on? Who has their video turned off? Who is dialing in by phone? There is a constellation between a live face, a frozen frame on camera, and a black spot with a telephone number in it. Constellations often can give us insight into unconscious bias and privilege and are, therefore, important to notice. Using chat on a video conference, for example, creates a constellation where participants calling in are marginalized by not being able to see the chat. What is the impact of that and how might you work with it?

Another way to see systems is to listen for metaphoric language in meetings to describe partnerships, teams, and workgroups. You can also ask team members to draw a picture or select an image that reflects their experience. If the team were an animal, car, city, country, or color, which one would it be? This helps the brain shifting from the analytical/strategic to the relational/creative.

Practical application: paper constellation

Think of a relationship system (for example, your team or a key stakeholder group) with an issue. Draw a large circle and place the members of the system in it. Start with yourself and see where you fit best (In the center? In the periphery?). Don't think too long about it; you intuitively know. Then place the other members in the system. You can also add forces/things/events that impact the relationship. Again, follow your intuition, most people know instantly how a particular system is constellated. Then make the connections between the key members using the key below.

```
KEY
Strong     ═══
Average    ───
Weak       ─ ─ ─ ─
Conflict   //

(example # represents an
average bond with a conflict)
```

Looking at the resulting constellation, what are you becoming aware of? This is a constellation of how you experience things in this moment. It often is a frustrating, difficult, or uncomfortable constellation. In constellations work, this is an important assessment. It sets the stage for you to create and innovate. We have consistently experienced that people were surprised, not only about how much they already knew, but also what they did not realize until they saw this picture emerge and got some "ah-ha" moments about what needs to change. That conversation sets the stage for the second constellation.

This is the moment of vision and more clarity about how to leverage locus of control so that it *could* be different and better. Draw the version of how you would like it to be. What are the shifts you need to make in this drawing for things to constellate differently? Allow yourself to be creative and make some changes.

Now, compare the constellations. What do you notice? What might be possible from this new constellation? Choose one or two actions that you can take in the next twenty-four hours to *begin to shift* the relationship in the direction of the second constellation.

Below is an example of a person considering her relationships with persons A, B, and C. Key insight was the need to involve person A more in the team. The key action was to set up a meeting with person A to get to know each other better and grow mutual understanding. Another action was to set up a meeting with all players to come closer together and grow as a team.

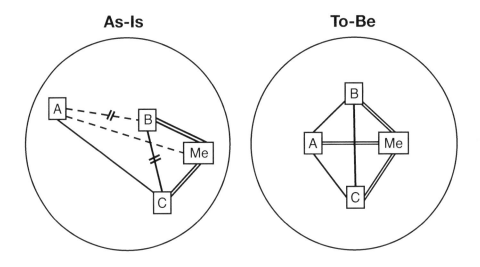

Quotes from the interviews

*"For most of us, this is a perceptual shift from seeing
individuals to seeing systems. We did not have
the language for it."*

- THE PRESIDENT OF A GLOBAL COACH TRAINING
AND CONSULTING COMPANY

*"It was fascinating to see how the same situation could be
perceived in different ways by different individuals in specific
situations. So, there is a lot more under the surface than
you initially assume."*

- THE HR EXECUTIVE OF A DIGITAL SCALE-UP

*"When you start talking with leaders about seeing their
organizations as living systems, they get that. Where does it
need some tender loving care? Where does it need a little
watering and where does it need a little pruning? What keeps
this system vibrant and what nourishes it?"*

- A RETIRED HEAD OF TRAINING OF A
GOVERNMENT DEPARTMENT

4. "Hear" the system: hold every voice as a voice of the system

As described in Chapter 3, when we discussed the principles of RSI, we hold that every voice in a relationship system is not only personal but also a voice or expression of the larger whole. A practical way to hear the system, therefore, is **to hold every voice first as "a voice of the system" rather than something personal. Combine this with the belief that all voices have a wisdom aspect, even the unpopular ones or the ones expressed unskillfully.** By doing so, more and different information can come to the surface, enabling you and your team to connect to the bigger picture. This supports skillful and efficient navigation of change and reduces resistance even when it gets challenging and hot. It helps to create insight into how the system is trying to evolve.

In the example of Alan Mulally of Ford: The unwillingness of people to share failures was an expression of fear and lack of trust in the system. These features belong to the system and are systemic expressions of the individuals involved. While each person's experience is personal, it is, first of all, an expression of the system. After facing that systemic event and team members were invited into the solution, the system could effectively see and hear itself. From that, a new culture could emerge in which problems could be shared and worked collectively!

There are many ways to implement this notion:

- In change initiatives, ensure that there are sufficient possibilities for input and feedback. For example, organize focus groups, do feedback rounds, create change agents in departments, and leverage the staff council.

- In task forces, ensure that members are a micro-cosmos of the bigger system so that the full range of voices is represented.

- Set up structures that enable everyone to participate. Consider using sticky notes for team members to put their observations, ideas, or challenges on a flip chart (or on tools like Jamboard or Miro when you work virtually). Processes like this allow the quieter, more introverted voices of the system to give input rather than being reduced by the louder, stronger voices.

Practical application: encourage dialog with questions

This technique is derived from an ancient Native American tradition. Once the topic is established, brainstorm with questions that do *not* have opinions embedded in them, for fifteen minutes. You can use random content questions that might start with, "What if...?". Within the first five minutes or so, one of two things will happen: members will run out of questions or will be offering solutions with a question mark! Allow the first, catch the second, and ask for a reframe of genuine curiosity asking the question you have no answers for. Questions usually will begin to flow again. After fifteen or twenty minutes, themes of possible solutions will emerge, often very different from what normally comes out of a strategic conversation. In most cases, this will provide the team with new, innovative directions to explore.

An example from Marita illustrates this approach. There was a conflict in a team around the process of communicating virtually. The team used to be office-based and very cohesive, but COVID-19 broke that way of working. It played out between two members in particular who were accusing one another of missed email responses and issues not communicated. And their behaviors shocked the team.

Marita asked all team members to think about how they are experiencing this issue in some form or fashion, given that everybody is working virtually now. She suggested viewing conflict as an unopened packet of information that has been thrown around under the label of "poor communication." And to consider that inside that packet might be useful information that now is getting dusty and dirty from all the kicking around. Then she introduced the technique of dialoguing with questions: "For the next fifteen minutes, we will only dialog in questions we do not have answers for. The focus will be on questions about what might be in that unopened packet of information that has been thrown around. This also is an exercise in building on and improvising from someone else's questions."

What followed were questions like: "What *is* in that packet? What if it is information about who we really are? What if it is information about new technology? What if it has nothing to do with communication? What if it *does* have to do with communication? What if it is about working at home? What if it is about not feeling connected?" Over the fifteen minutes, she kept track of the emerging themes in the questions. This is what showed up:

- Communication when we are not in the office

- What is missing when working from home?

- What is missing in technology?

- Feeling disconnected

When she shared these themes, there was an immediate exhale, and they started talking about the loss of connection and the frustration of only communicating via email. The team identified two big themes:

- Lack of connection and sense of belonging

- Frustration with their existing technology

These then became the key areas to work on for the team. The session ended with the two individuals reflecting on themselves. For the first time, they realized they were actually a voice of the system. They thought it was about them, but it was in fact a systemic issue! The rest of the team thanked them for being brave enough to raise it and for the trust they felt in the team to have the argument in the first place!

Quotes from the interviews

"When someone says something, I learned that they're not speaking on behalf of themselves but of the system."

- THE TECHNICAL SERVICES MANAGER
OF AN ENERGY COMPANY

"Making sure that all the voices are heard is I think what I do most often. It seems little but does make a difference."

- THE SENIOR AGILE MANAGER OF
A GLOBAL CONSULTANCY

"I am quite sensitive about quiet voices and encourage them to speak up."

- THE CHIEF OPERATING OFFICER OF A TRIBUNAL

5. "Sense" the system: track and work with the energy/emotional field

In Systems Inspired Leadership, we pay a lot of attention to how people feel and experience things. Quite specific is our focus on monitoring changes in the atmosphere or type of energy of a relationship system at any given moment in time. We refer to these as "shifts in the emotional field." This is a very rich source of information that is often forgotten as we are so focused on the content. It provides important "footprints" and snapshots about the invisible experience of the system and is an expression of what is important, challenging, difficult, and life-giving for the team at any given moment. A significant percentage of what drives decision-making happens at this invisible and often unconscious level of experience. And over time, these emotional fields are an important aspect of what becomes known as the "culture" of a team.

Many of you might have had the experience of walking into a restaurant you have not visited before, and somehow it did not feel welcoming, or for some unknown reason, you turned around and walked out. Chances are that you unconsciously responded to the emotional field within that restaurant. Or, you walk into a meeting, and the moment you enter the door, you can feel something is off. Same greetings as usual, but there is something in the atmosphere—even if you cannot put your finger on it—that is different. *That* is what is known as "sensing" the system and working with the emotional field. Bringing conscious awareness to it is critical for resolution, team performance, and efficacy.

For a Systems Inspired Leader, it is important to notice and work with these shifts. It is key to reveal them to the system and make them the subject of conversation. From systems theory, we know that once the system is revealed to itself, it has the potential for knowing how to self-correct or re-direct itself. By slowing down and reflecting on what has just happened, the system becomes aware of itself and can make conscious choices to change and break old patterns. Working with the emotional field is an important subset of revealing the system to itself that we will discuss in-depth in Chapter 7.

For many leaders, it is initially challenging to work with the emotional field. Firstly, as we are often so immersed in the content that we forget about energy shifts in the room. Like someone in the interviews said: *"At the beginning, it was a little bit like holding a piece of a slippery soap. I would go into a meeting with the intention to observe what is happening in the emotional field. And then it just slips away, and after the meeting, I think I had it, I had it, I lost it."*

Matthew Lieberman from UCLA gave a good explanation for this in his book *Social: Why Our Brains Are Wired to Connect.* He found that we have two distinct thinking networks in our brain: one for analytical thinking and one for social thinking. They serve as a neural seesaw: if one is active, the other gets quieter. In other words, if we are heavily immersed in content discussions, then it will be harder to recognize the social/relationship dynamics at play. And when the brain becomes fatigued in analytical thinking, one of the ways to restore and rest is to shift to social thinking and engagement. Conscious and intentional ways to dance between these two are known to create greater team efficacy.

The second reason that many leaders find working with the emotional field challenging resides in the old belief that feelings and emotions do not belong in the workplace. It is simply not professional to show them, let alone to talk about them. We believe this is a fallacy. As we said before, humans are, first of all, emotional beings. Additionally, emotions are the currency of relationships. Tracking them and working with them is powerful and helps the system evolve. In 2009, James Zenger published a study in which he found that combining *results focus* and *social skills* skyrocketed the perceived leadership of a person, from respectively 14 percent (results focus) and 12 percent (social skills) to 72 percent when those two were combined!

The third reason is that you may feel it slows down the process. You have a concern that no progress is made on the content side. We want to challenge this. Shifts in the emotional field are indicators that something important is happening, and reflecting this will help the system to break recurring patterns and move forward on a structural basis. It is slowing down, to go faster.

In this context, it is also valuable to look at employee engagement. Disengagement is rampant globally in many organizations. For example, Gallup reported in 2020 that only 36 percent of employees in the USA are engaged and 14 percent are actively disengaged. So, more than six out of ten employees are disengaged and a significant proportion of them do so actively.

Disengagement is an emotional response of the system with a huge impact on productivity and quality and is often attempted to be "fixed" with structural changes such as incentives/rewards and recognition programs. As outlined in the 2019 Deloitte's Human Capital Trends report, it would be better to pay attention to the "human experience" and to create an experience that is both "bottom-up and personal." It is about "building on an understanding of worker aspirations [in order] to connect work back to the impact it will have on helping people achieve their aspirations." These notions align very well with Systems Inspired Leadership.

Practical applications

- Pay attention to the "atmosphere" or "feel" in different parts of the room. Emotional fields are like pockets of weather. It might feel cloudy for a section of the team, while it might be sunnier in a different part. It is one of the reasons it is important to bring attention to this since the emotional field plays such a huge role in decision making and alignment. Describe, and have the team describe, in a neutral way what it is like. Asking for a weather report from the team is a way of doing that! Parts of the team will experience some thunder and lightning, other parts may be in a foggy place and yet others might experience some rain showers.

These are the invisible and unconscious experiences impacting all team members and from which all team members engage and contribute. It is important to educate teams about this and normalize the different experiences in different parts of the system. All are critical elements of the collective experience of the team. Revealing these, normalizing them as part of systemic functioning, and working directly with them, is a great way to co-create Systems Inspired Safety (see also Chapter 9).

- As indicated above, when working with the emotional field, it is important not to interpret what you experience but to use neutral language. Ask open-ended questions (like, "What is happening right now? What are you becoming aware of?") and let the team find their own words to express the experience. In **Appendix 2,** you can find 40 ways to read and work with the emotional field.

- In team meetings, leaders often come up against a place where the team is simply stuck and cannot, or will not, move into action. The Systems Inspired Leader will explore this invisible but powerful field by remarking about it and inviting the team into exploring the experience. Embody and identify with being stuck and even deepen it. The more it is resisted, the more it will be amplified. Invite conversations between the "stuck" side and another option. Normalizing these events supports the systemic evolution. Very often, this kind of experience is about the emergence of a new way forward that feels simply too edgy to entertain. Exploring and navigating this, together with the team, opens different gates to insight and action that was shrouded by a certain amount of fear and challenge.

Quotes from the interviews

"Attention to the emotional field is another one of those counter-intuitive things that are going to make people better at their job, more productive, happier."

- THE FINANCE DIRECTOR OF A HEALTH SERVICES AGENCY

"It is as if an invisible curtain is put on the emotional field. Everyone is aware of it but no one will articulate it. It is still unconscious. It is a very strange phenomenon."

- THE DIRECTOR OF A LOCAL COACH TRAINING AND CONSULTING COMPANY

6. Educate your team/organization on Relationship Systems Intelligence and Systems Inspired Leadership

Share with your team why you do what you do as a Systems Inspired Leader, not only for them to understand your approach better, but also to invite them to take their seat at the table and become co-responsible for leadership as you navigate through unavoidable emerging changes. Educate them about relationship systems, 3rd entity, the importance of shifting the focus from the parts to the whole, seeing and hearing systems, sensing the emotional field, and (the principles of) Relationship Systems Intelligence. Do this with a light touch, one piece at a time, and, ideally, while creating in the moment. With repetition and an increased experience of collaboration and team efficacy, this will impact the culture not only of your team but the entire organization. Consider organizing specific training sessions, which will lead to a different understanding of teaming and create a common language and lens for working together. Collectively, there is a natural evolution into a more self-organizing team where members step up and take on the leadership role rather than relying on the leader to hold that space and come up with the answers.

Quote from the interviews

"I developed an educational piece, about the why (contextual framework), the principles, the model, and tools. And in this way helping them to become systems leaders as well."

- A CUSTOMER OPERATIONS MANAGER
OF A MAJOR MULTINATIONAL

ASSESS YOURSELF ON THIS COMPETENCY

- Rate yourself on a scale from 1 to 5 on the following beliefs and behaviors, where 1 means "I never do this," 3 means "I do this regularly," and 5 means "I do this all the time." [You can also use the digital assessment mentioned on the bonus page at the end of this book.]

- Add up the scores and determine how strong you are in this competency:

  - Between 10-20: you are becoming aware of this competency.

  - Between 20-30: you are developing skills in this competency.

  - Between 30-40: you are skilled in this competency.

  - Between 40-50: you are masterful in this competency.

- Now, determine what you would like to work on, using the ideas and practices of this chapter as input.

1. I see a relationship system as a living organism with its own wisdom.	....
2. I can hold a meta-view, shifting the gaze from the individual to the whole system.	....
3. When I hear the contributions/reactions of my team members, I consider them as both personal and a voice of the system.	....

4. If someone is not performing, I consider the personal as well as the systemic reasons for this.	....
5. I regularly invite my team or colleagues to stand in the shoes of the relationship system and speak the "system's view."	....
6. I regularly—on a piece of paper—map myself in relation to my team members or key stakeholders to get a better view of what is happening in the system.	....
7. I believe that all voices of the relationship system need to be heard, including the unpopular ones.	....
8. I hear the wisdom aspect of each voice, even if expressed unskillfully.	....
9. In meetings, I sense shifts in the energy or atmosphere of the system and reflect them back.	....
10. I regularly educate my team about relationship systems and relationship systems intelligence.	....

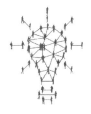

CHAPTER 6

DOING – HOLDING CONSCIOUS AND INTENTIONAL RELATIONSHIP

"The work we do is all about relationships. We're not helping people to do their job. We're helping them how to be in their job, and how to be with others; it's relationship work. And that's the piece I think that is absolutely missing now in many organizations."

- THE LEADERSHIP DEVELOPMENT LEAD OF A GLOBAL TECHNOLOGY COMPANY

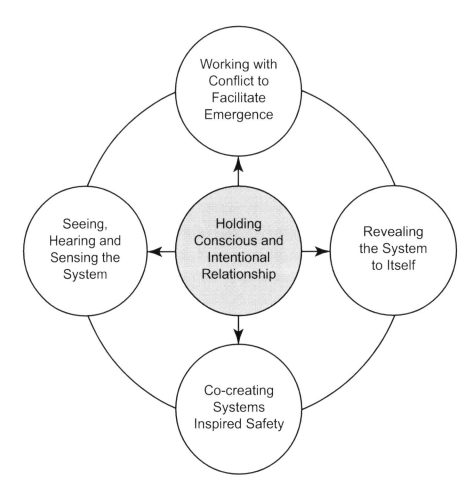

Definition of "Holding Conscious and Intentional Relationship"

Ability to create conscious and intentional relationships by

- choosing upfront and rehearsing how you want to show up as a leader (your "come from" place)

- co-designing how to be together in a relationship system, including when things get difficult

- adjusting the energy you bring during a meeting based on what the relationship system needs at any given moment in time

Link with Relationship Systems Intelligence (RSI)

While acknowledging that the RSI principles are interdependent and interconnected, the following principles link particularly well with this competency:

- Every member of a relationship system is a "voice of the system."

- Relationship systems rely on roles for their organization and execution of functions. Roles belong to the system, not just the individuals that inhabit the role within the system. Being conscious and intentional helps to create the role fluidity required for systems to thrive.

Ways to grow this competency

In this chapter, we discuss five powerful ways to help you advance this competency:

1. Practice conscious and intentional relationships with self and others.

2. Choose and rehearse your MetaSkills.

3. Design the Team Alliance.

4. Model co-responsibility.

5. Slowing down.

1. *Practice conscious and intentional relationships with self and others*

Creating conscious and intentional relationship is at the core of Systems Inspired Leadership. We, therefore, put it at the heart of the competency model. It builds an important bridge between the "doing" and "being" aspects of your leadership and is crucial for developing excellent soft skills. We also call this creating right relationship. "Right" here does not refer to the traditional "right or wrong." It is about being present and choosing consciously and intentionally who you want to be, both as an individual and as a team. It is about bringing to bear integrity and personal and organizational/social values to how you want to appear in a particular situation.

Research shows that this is critical for high performance:

- In 2019, IBM published the outcomes of a survey of 5800 executives across 50 countries. They found that the biggest skills gaps are not technical/digital skills but soft skills, like a willingness to be flexible, agile, and adaptable to change; an ability to work effectively in team environments; and the ability to communicate. In other words, the soft skills have become the hard (more difficult) skills for organizations and leaders.

- A study by Carnegie Mellon, MIT, and Union College in 2010 on collective intelligence showed that groups exceeded the cognitive abilities of individual group members. Having a bunch of smart people in a group does not necessarily make the group smart. The key distinguishing factor for collective intelligence was "social sensitivity," so how well group members perceive each other's emotions. Another important factor was the extent to which conversational turns were more evenly distributed rather than people dominating.

- As discussed in Chapter 5, Matthew Lieberman (UCLA) identified two distinct thinking networks in our brain: one for analytical
  thinking, the other for social thinking. He discovered that they
  serve as a neural seesaw: if one is active, the other gets quieter. If
  there are more analytical discussions, then it will be harder to recognize the social issues at play and vice versa. In other words, our
  brains make it difficult to be both socially and analytically focused
  at the same time. Given the dominance of analytical thinking in
  most organizations, it is at the expense of social/soft skills. It is,
  therefore, very effective to put your conscious attention there.

These studies confirm the importance of being conscious and intentional and building right relationships. This leads to better outcomes, for
yourself, your colleagues, and your team/organization. Great teams and
organizations do not happen by accident. They happen consciously and
intentionally.

Creating right relationship is dependent on the context of the relationship system and a function of what people want to achieve together.
The task and people/relationship sides are strongly interwoven, they are
two sides of the same coin. One of our interviewees phrased this as follows:
"We work on right relationship in service of what we want to achieve
together. This is not just about being nice to each other." We believe that
each relationship system has a higher purpose, an essence that wants to
manifest itself in the world. Right relationship is pivotal for this, enabling
relationship systems to thrive and achieve extraordinary results.

This is also about honoring when a relationship might be over. It could,
for example, be better for an individual to leave a system/organization or
for a team to dissolve (with high integrity and respect, of course). Recognizing the truth in that is another—sometimes painful version—of being in
right relationship. While it may be difficult for the individuals involved, from

the meta-view of "systems are in a constant state of emergence," it could be a normal emerging systemic event.

A good example can be found in nature. California Redwoods propagate and grow when they burn down. That is what is allowing new growth. The same applies to systems we are part of. Because of this, one of the things we say to our leaders and coaches is: "You can help an elephant that is trying to get up. You may not be able to help an elephant that is trying to fall down." Part of the challenge of being a Systems Inspired Leader is to hold awareness of the nature and flow of systemic evolution. What wants to be left alone, or to be put to rest? What is viable, and wants to grow? These are the moments to remember that leadership is a role that belongs to the system. Invite team members into these conversations and honor their views as leadership input. The final decision will be yours, but it is executed very differently from that shared view.

Quotes from the interviews

"It is about right relationships, so not about nice relationships. It's about showing up who you are and about alignment. How can we work together?"

- THE CEO OF AN EXECUTIVE AND
SYSTEMS COACHING COMPANY

"It is right relationship, for this system, in this moment, for this purpose."

- THE LEADERSHIP DEVELOPMENT LEAD OF
A GLOBAL TECHNOLOGY COMPANY

2. Choose and rehearse your Metaskills

A powerful way to create conscious and intentional relationships is by choosing your Metaskills. This term was coined by Amy Mindell in her book *Metaskills: The Spiritual Art of Therapy* and refers to the feeling quality that brings your skills to life and makes them more effective. What is your stance, attitude, "come from place" in any given situation? What is the energetic impact you want to make on the system? What is your intention? What is the atmosphere you want to create? What emotional field would serve this system best? What is the desired culture you want to seed the room with while you are working on a task or outcome? For example, you can choose to be welcoming if you are the host of an event. You can choose to be open to influence when someone wants to discuss a difficult issue with you.

Metaskills are not fixed. You choose them, depending on what is needed for a particular event or in a particular moment. It intentionally "perfumes" the room in service of the objectives of the meeting or event, to enhance the impact. It helps you to create from a situation rather than to react. There is an endless number of Metaskills possible, depending on what serves the relationship system best (see **Appendix 3** for a list of 120 useful Metaskills).

Below, we highlight seven Metaskills that are particularly powerful for building conscious and intentional relationship and creating sustainability:

HEART	being empathetic, bringing warmth, and understanding
DEEP DEMOCRACY	Honoring that all voices in a system are important and bring wisdom
PLAYFULNESS	Bringing lightness and positivity

RESPECT	Accepting others as valuable human beings
COLLABORATION/ PARTNERSHIP	Willingness to work together
CURIOSITY	Willingness to explore and learn, creating new awareness
COMMITMENT	Showing that you want to achieve something together

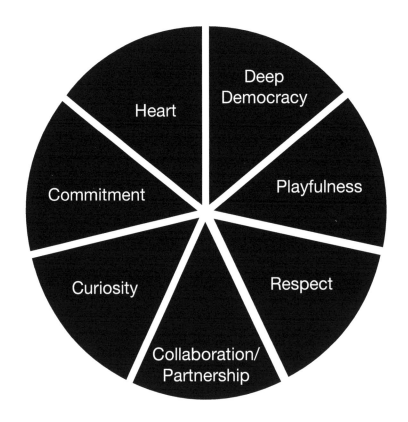

When delivering our training or practice, we always have a pre-discussion in the morning as the leader team. We connect with the material and reflect on where the participants might be and what they might need. Then we ask what Metaskills would serve them best and choose those. This can be playfulness, heart, rigor, challenge, or curiosity—whatever we feel will serve the system best. Sometimes, we will make a movement together to experience it even stronger. It is an embodied way to fill the room with this energy and to anchor the Metaskills in ourselves.

Practical application

- As a Systems Inspired Leader, choose your Metaskills consciously and intentionally. Take a minute to reflect before every meeting: What is my intention for this meeting? What is the attitude I want to bring to the meeting? How do I want to show up? You may not always be able to fully deliver on this intention (we are all human), but at least there is a higher chance that you are how you want to be and become more impactful. And it is not extra work; it is about becoming conscious and intentional in your being and allow that beingness to enhance your doing. Rehearsing is an important element of it. We often get so immersed in the conversation that we forget about our intentions.

- Request your team members to do the same. To keep the Metaskill(s) in the forefront, ask each team member to put it on a sticky name tag and wear it for the duration of the meeting. When team members work remotely, ask them to add it to their screen name or put it on a post-it note. This is a powerful way to create co-responsibility and become custodians for Metaskills.

Quotes from the interviews

"If I'm going to a meeting, a difficult conversation, or an event, I always reflect upfront how I want to be and what is needed from me to address the issues at hand."

- FOUNDING PARTNER OF A REGIONAL
COACHING AND TRAINING COMPANY

*"When I see there is something lacking in the system, I try to bring that. When there is too much seriousness, I bring that lightness. When there is too much lightness,
I bring that seriousness."*

- THE REGIONAL HR DIRECTOR OF A
GLOBAL TRADING COMPANY

3. Design the Team Alliance (DTA)

One of the most powerful ways to build conscious and intentional relationships is to Design the Team Alliance (DTA). This is about designing a "social contract" with your team to be more collaborative in a specific meeting while you are tackling the challenges of the task at hand. In order to do that, the task at hand must be paused while doing the DTA. It is not the same as designing an action plan and outcomes for the task. Rather, it creates the culture within which you will be able to thrive as a team even when things get difficult. It is not the same as a team charter as it is a living alliance. The DTA will be created at the beginning, and it remains a work in progress as teams prototype the best ways of being together when working on the task at hand. Being conscious and intentional in this process provides a powerful vehicle for building organizational culture. Over time, certain aspects of the DTA will turn into values. For example, when facing disagreement, a DTA intention to be "open to be influenced" will carry across multiple and different task agendas and become part of the team culture.

Designing the Team Alliance is the most frequently used tool amongst global alumni, practitioners, and leaders and is a critical part of the meeting for a Systems Inspired Leader. It centers around three questions that are asked after the objectives and agenda of the meeting have been explained:

- What atmosphere/culture do we want to create together to achieve the objectives of the meeting?

- How do we want to be when things get difficult?

  This question is particularly helpful since it normalizes human and systemic behavior of challenge and disagreement. And this will happen! When it does, "What might be the best way to work with it, given who we are together?" is one of the most powerful questions a leader can ask the team. Doing this upfront provides the team with attitudes and behaviors that will allow them to press the pause button and design how to be together when this happens. This would otherwise be hard.

- What will help us to excel and be masterful?

  You will find a DTA example on the next page.

DTA example from the field (created on Zoom)

DTA
(Designing the Team Alliance)

Atmosphere & Culture

Confidentially	Respect	Challenge	Playfulness

When Difficult

Openness – Invite Other Voices	Listening With An Open Heart	Be Curious	Assume Positive Intent

Excelling/Being Masterful

Supporting and Encouraging Each Other	Authenticity – Be Who You Are	Flow	Learning Mindset

The final action is to create accountability for the delivery of the alliance. Ask team members to choose one or two elements of the team alliance for which they will take responsibility. Make sure to tap them for it and demonstrate the need for them to bring it to the table. (e.g., openness, respect, or fun).

Next, you design how the team wants to work with you as their System Inspired Leader and the leader alliance. (See the illustration on the following page.) The questions are basically the same: "How do you want me to be with you? What expectations do we have of each other? What will help our partnership to thrive?" This is also a great place to design how you as a leader want to express your own point of view and how you use your decision-making power. As you will see in Chapter 11 (Implementing Systems Inspired Leadership), it became clear in the interviews that many find it challenging to combine the role of facilitator and decision-maker. The fact you hold hierarchical power has an impact and it is better to design around that.

It is helpful to put the team and leader alliance on a flip chart (or on tools like Jamboard or Miro when you work virtually), so it is transparent for everyone and you can refer to it. Get a few notes down under each of the headings/questions. Remember the first time around it is "made up," so not yet informed by actual experience.

The biggest challenges with using the DTA are a) that you spend too much time with it and b) that you do not follow up. It can be done fast (e.g., by asking: "Is there anything we want to design together?") or take some time (e.g., thirty minutes), depending on the meeting at hand and the experience of the group. Empirical evidence from the field shows that the more this concept is kept alive and evolved, the more the team is creating a culture that significantly improves team efficacy.

While the benefits of this tool are numerous, we still notice that there is sometimes reluctance to use it. For some, this step feels unnecessary and slow. People are so used to jumping into the content straight away. In our experience, the payback of the investment is huge as you address potential issues upfront and create the organizational culture you want. It is another example of going slow in order to go fast.

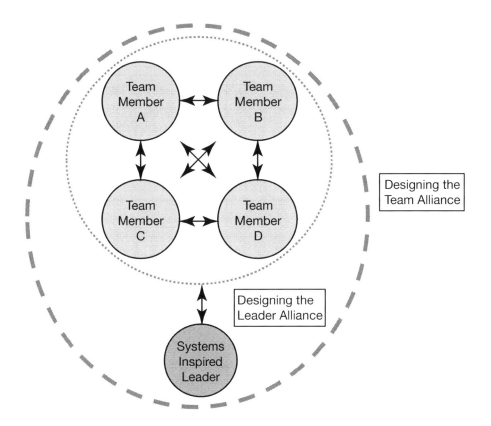

Practical application

- **The form and function of the team alliance can also be applied to other systems.** For example, you can **design the team alliance with your individual team members**. Have an upfront conversation with them about the atmosphere in which you want to work together, including when things get difficult, and then review it from time to time. This could be a natural addition to the logistical elements you may discuss: "Will we use fixed dates for our one-on-ones? How long will they take? What is the standard agenda? How do we connect with each other in an emergency? How to deal with bad news?" In this way, you tailor your leadership to the individual needs of your team members. It will save you lots of time. We so often see issues between people that could have been prevented if there was a designed alliance in place.

Quotes from the interviews

"And in the first meeting as a group, we designed our alliance, how we want to be together, what we commit to each other. Wow, you felt the shift in the emotional field; it really bonded us as a team!"

- THE DIRECTOR OF TALENT MANAGEMENT
OF A MAJOR MULTINATIONAL

"[Designing the Team Alliance] has significantly transformed my leadership, because I invite people to design how they are going to interact with each other, which is empowering. And I also invite them to co-design with me what my leadership looks like."

- THE OWNER OF A REGIONAL EXECUTIVE
AND TEAM COACHING COMPANY

"As a leader, I ask: 'What do you need from me? How can I support you?' And this is a living thing, so we may have a situation that we haven't designed for, but we have a tool to design in the moment."

- THE DIRECTOR OF TALENT MANAGEMENT
OF A MAJOR MULTINATIONAL

4. Model co-responsibility

When something goes wrong, it is easy to point the finger at someone else or at another department. "It is their fault." **A Systems Inspired Leader knows that they must focus first on their own role in the situation.** "Given that systems are interdependent, how did I contribute to what has happened and what can I do to change the situation?"

Frank once worked with a team in which there was a difficult relationship between two team members. He reflected that this is an issue for the entire team. Given that the others did not intervene and only contributed to the status quo. He got an emotional phone call the next day from one of the team members saying that it was unfair to say this as this was really something between these two individuals. This can be seen as an unwillingness to accept co-responsibility. Such a reaction is understandable since, for many, it will take time to evolve to a more systemic point of view.

This notion of co-responsibility is both sobering and empowering. It's sobering since you always bear some responsibility for what has happened—empowering because you have always the possibility to influence the system. Your personal change counts. If you change, the system will change. By owning the "2 percent truth" of what might have been your blind spot, you do not only change the system, you also create the safety for others to own their failings and create new learning from that. Like Mahatma Gandhi said, "Be the change you want to see."

Practical applications

- In case of failures, mistakes, or problematic relationships, reflect on the question of how you might have contributed to the situation and what you could do differently. Talk about this openly with your team and build learning from there.

- During a challenging change initiative (e.g., implementing more diversity and inclusion in your organization), ask yourself and your team how we may have a blind spot for what needs to change and how each of us may unwittingly be one of the blockers.

Quotes from the interviews

"The relationship systems approach made me become better aligned with the adult-self inside of me. I now take full responsibility for my life; the victim side is far away."

- A DIRECTOR OF A LOCAL COACH TRAINING
AND CONSULTING COMPANY

"Even if I'm extremely confident that I'm right, it does not matter. It is just really a snippet of the whole story."

- A CUSTOMER OPERATIONS MANAGER OF
A MAJOR MULTINATIONAL

5. Slowing down

This is an important skill for a Systems Inspired Leader and quite challenging in high-paced environments and stressful situations. The speed of change is often so high that it is easy to slip into a reactive mode. As speech gets louder and dialogs happen faster, it often initiates fight or flight responses within us and our people. As we saw in the Lieberman study, it is important then to disengage from the "analytical/strategic" mind and return to the "social/relationship mind" to recover. It is only by slowing down that deeply engrained patterns become visible and insights emerge that creates sustainable change, and in this way, it converts the speed of change into the speed of evolution.

Practical applications for slowing down

- **For self:** when under pressure or becoming reactive, take a break or create mini pauses. The four seconds rule may serve you: take one deep breath before you act. This may turn a reaction into a response.

- **For a team:** when getting stuck or encountering something awkward, take a break in silence, and ask team members to explore what was trying to emerge. Let them write notes about it, and consider using an object that exemplifies or is a metaphor for the challenge. When the team gets back together in small groups, share notes and group them into themes. Put the object they chose in front to dialog together about it. Trust this is a worthwhile investment that will bring important new information to the surface, enabling you to break hard patterns. All of this is not only slowing them down, but it also is taking them out of linear mind allowing different insights to populate the conversation.

Quotes from the interviews

"Slowing down is counterintuitive because everything speeds up and pressure increases. We are trying to do more, but we have to find time in our day to slow down, reflect, and really get in touch with ourselves and whatever mechanism that is for people. It is learning a new skill that is so intrinsically different from how we operate in a command-and-control world. There is magic in slowing down."

- A CUSTOMER OPERATIONS MANAGER
OF A MAJOR MULTINATIONAL

"We slow down to create a foundation to really go fast. Yes, it is at the expense of speed initially, but really what unfolds is that it moves with the speed at which the system can go."

- A MANAGING PARTNER OF REGIONAL
COACHING AND TRAINING COMPANY

ASSESS YOURSELF ON THIS COMPETENCY

- Rate yourself on a scale from 1 to 5 on the following beliefs and behaviors, where 1 means "I never do this," 3 means "I do this regularly," and 5 means "I do this all the time." [You can also use the digital assessment mentioned on the bonus page at the end of this book.]

- Add up the scores and determine how strong you are in this competency:

  - Between 10-20: you are becoming aware of this competency.

  - Between 20-30: you are developing skills in this competency.

  - Between 30-40: you are skilled in this competency.

  - Between 40-50: you are masterful in this competency.

- Now, determine what you would like to work on, using the ideas and practices of this chapter as input.

1. I reflect upfront and rehearse how I want to show up to a specific meeting and request the same from my team.	··········
2. I co-design upfront with a relationship system on how to be together to achieve certain business/meeting objectives.	··········

3. I co-design upfront with a relationship system on how to be together when things get difficult.	....
4. I co-design upfront on how the relationship system wants to work with me as a leader, and I am willing to be vulnerable here.	....
5. I invest the time required to design and review how we want to work together rather than jumping straight into the content."	....
6. I adjust the energy I bring to a meeting, based on my conscious perception of what the system needs in any given moment.	....
7. If relationships are challenging/problematic, I explore how I contributed to them and invite others to do the same.	....
8. If I want things to go differently in my team/organization, I actively explore what I might need to change in myself to accomplish this.	....
9. I hold leadership to be a role that belongs to the system and not just to me.	....
10. I am comfortable asking for help and input from the system and do not assume I have all the answers.	....

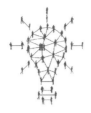

CHAPTER 7

DOING – REVEALING THE SYSTEM TO ITSELF

"It is a different way to solve problems or conflict. There is a sense that looking at it together and reveal the system to itself will help to catalyze something new."

- THE OWNER OF A REGIONAL EXECUTIVE AND TEAM COACHING COMPANY

Definition of "Revealing the System to Itself"

- Ability to "mirror" what is happening or trying to happen in a relationship system in order to create systemic self-awareness and enable conscious choice and "self-correction."

- Ability to make the invisible visible and the unconscious conscious.

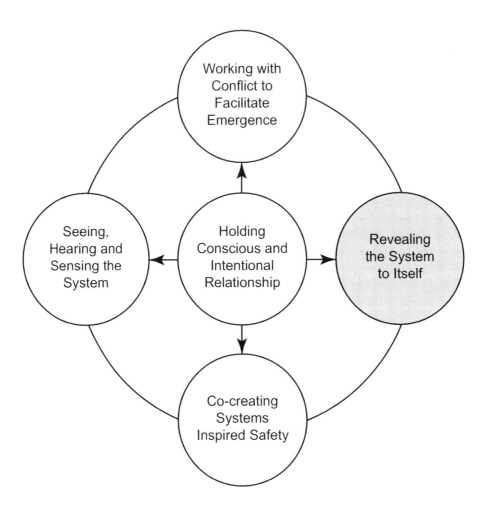

Link with Relationship Systems Intelligence (RSI)

While acknowledging that the RSI principles are interdependent and interconnected, the following principles link particularly well with this competency:

- Relationship systems are naturally intelligent, generative, and creative.

- Relationship systems are in a constant state of emergence, always in the process of expressing their potential.

The focus of a Systems Inspired Leader is on what is trying to happen in a relationship system and working *with* the system on emergence and change rather than reacting to it or imposing change top-down.

Ways to grow this competency

In this chapter, we discuss five powerful ways to help you advance this competency:

1. Revealing the system to itself is your superpower!

2. Use the edge model as a lens to navigate change and facilitate emergence.

3. Monitor the ground conditions for change.

4. Be neutral when revealing the system to itself.

5. Remember that change is an emotional journey.

1. Revealing the system to itself is your superpower!

Revealing the system to itself is one of the core functions of a Systems Inspired Leader. It invites the team to create from any change the system is experiencing and to leverage its intelligence, creativity, and wisdom. From the relationship systems perspective, once the system is revealed to itself, new information enters the system, making the system self-aware and activating its natural ability to self-correct. Revealing the system to itself makes the invisible visible, the unconscious conscious, and opens the possibility to create answers and solutions together, leveraging the collective whole rather than working with just the individual voices.

This is a very different approach than used by "hero leaders," the ones who know it all and impose their answers on the system. It is also why leaders in our research found Systems Inspired Leadership so attractive. The weight/burden of responsibility shifts from *one* leader to all, creating space for all to contribute. Responsibility is held by all and becomes something much more alive and creative. It is about leveraging the intelligence and experience of everyone, freeing you from having to be a leader with all the answers. Indeed, leadership has become a team sport!

Revealing can take many forms. In organizations, a lot of attention is usually given to the analytical side of revealing. Think of the monthly, quarterly, or annual reviews, the dashboards, the scorecards. Together you can review key performance indicators (KPIs), customer feedback, employee surveys, policy documents, 360 feedback. Summarizing, asking powerful questions, sharing learning, and giving feedback are also powerful ways of revealing the system to itself. And more and more advanced modeling technology will become available to simulate complex systems and get an idea of the (intended and unintended) consequences of potential interventions. Systems Inspired Leaders will use all the above.

In addition, they pay special attention to hearing, seeing, and sensing the system (Chapter 5). This is about looking at the experiential side, reflecting how people feel and experience things in the moment. It is working with what is happening in the here and now rather than reviewing past data. Simply revealing this is a powerful intervention in itself. By creating self-awareness, the Systems Inspired Leader trusts the systemic notion of self-regulating: the natural ability of systems to self-correct when able to see and experience themselves.

All Systems Inspired Leadership tools are designed to reveal the system to itself, produce new information that disrupts the current thinking, and give the system new insights and choices for action. They support the system to give birth to something new and facilitate emergence.

The easiest and most common way to reveal the system to itself is to **hear** all voices on a subject. Systems Inspired Leaders value diversity of input, encourage out-of-the-box thinking, and in so doing, leverage conversations of creativity from which more informed action can be taken. They make sure that there is room for all voices, including the less popular ones. The Metaskill of Deep Democracy *("all voices count")* and the systems inspired rule (*everyone is right... partially*) are always present and breathing through the conversations.

This revealing the system to itself can be reinforced by adding a visual component to it, to **see** the system. This is not (yet) common in the board room. It helps to make the conversation less "heady" and create an experience. Some examples:

- *Polling:* e.g., show with your thumbs what you think about a proposal. Thumb up means fully in favor; thumb down means not at all in favor; thumb somewhere in between reflects the degree of being in favor. Within a few seconds, you get a visual representation of the system in the room. You then ask people to clarify their point of view and build action from there. You can also use word clouds and other interactive presentation software here.

- *Constellations:* you can ask people to position themselves in a room relative to a topic and start revealing. Frank remembers the example of an organization with a work-life balance issue. He wrote the topic "Work-Life Balance" on a piece of paper and put it in the middle of the (empty) room and then asked people to constellate around it. If your work-life balance is very good, you stand close to the paper. Otherwise, you stand far away. If it is somewhere in between, you position yourself accordingly. People distributed themselves. Most were around the center, some were halfway, and one person was very far away. And only seeing this resulting constellation was impactful and revealing. People were shocked. They had not realized that it was so severe for this person. It created a visceral experience of how work-life balance lived in their system and why it was needed to address it. The geography part of this tool (moving around in the room) helped significantly to create this experience. He then asked people to constellate around the question of how active they were in creating a better work-life balance and how active they would like to be. This gave rise to a rich conversation and solid action planning, both at the collective and individual level.

This experience can easily be done virtually by asking people to position themselves with a sticky note using apps like Jamboard or Miro (see example below).

Rick

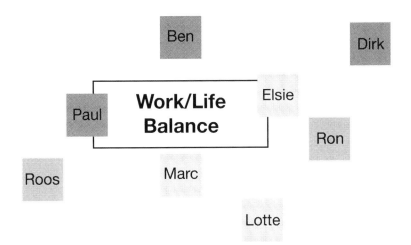

- *Wheel:* this is a special constellation. There are many applications and variations possible, so you can be creative here! For example, you can explore how you, as a team, embody the company values. Put a wheel on the floor with tape (the number of wedges depends on how many you need for an exercise). Ask people to stand in the wedge/value they feel is most embodied by the team. Make the team aware of the resulting constellation, and then ask them to say why they chose their spot. In the next round, ask them to stand in the wedge/value that is least embodied in the team and repeat the process. This will create a rich conversation from which powerful learnings and actions can be drawn. You can use tools like Jamboard and Miro to enable these conversations when working virtually.

- *Picture:* ask people to draw a picture or select an image that best represents how they feel right now, for example, about a reorganization. Look at the pictures together, and let everyone speak, noting common themes.

- *Metaphoric language*: encourage people to use metaphoric language ("What's the metaphor for this?"), e.g., "This project is like a roller coaster." Or: "I feel we are stuck in the mud right now."

During meetings, the Systems Inspired Leader is constantly **sensing** the system, tracking shifts in the energy/emotional field. What is happening in the moment? Is it tense, confusing, or relaxed? Is there laughter, excitement, or silence? These are the unconscious footprints of the actual systemic experience. Systems Inspired Leaders will neutrally reflect these shifts to the system and support and invite others to do the same. Inquiring about that experience in the room, and what is underneath it, will help create awareness of what is not consciously experienced, which is frequently actually driving decision-making.

Revealing the system to itself is a way of slowing down (Chapter 6). It is moving out of the reactive mode and pressing the pause button to see what is actually going on in the system, and what is trying to happen. It is from there that something new can emerge.

Practical application: organizational lands work

This exercise is based on one of the most popular tools in our relationship systems and team coaching training. It combines hearing, seeing, and sensing the system. Its purpose is to create more understanding and alignment between departments (which are considered "lands" in the exercise) through stepping into the experience of different teams. Different departments focus on different outcomes and are impacted by challenges and experiences unique to their goals and desired outcomes. The ability to step into that experience is what opens the door to a whole new understanding and ability for collaboration. Organizational Lands Work is a powerful tool to break silos and provides a deeper recognition of the need for Emotional and Social Intelligence to understand and honor the diversity of their experience. An important step in this process is shifting their system to RSI allowing them to feel into, reflect on, and co-author with the system itself to learn how to emerge more prepared and unified and shift into what needs to happen from these insights. Empirical evidence from the field shows that integrating the land metaphor into the organizational language helps to create a culture shift. You may hear, "How are things in your land? What is happening in your land? Responding to your request, in my land…" The language of "lands" often enables a deeper and richer conversation than the standard organizational language.

- Make a wheel on the floor with as many wedges as the number of departments (see an example of three lands below). Everybody stands in their department's land. Take some time to talk together about your land.

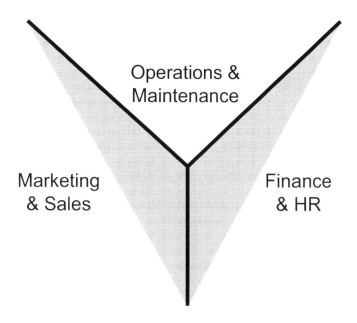

Operations &
Maintenance

Marketing
& Sales

Finance
& HR

- Phase 1: Interview questions for members in their own land.

  · What do you love about your department?

  · What is difficult in your land?

  · What do you want members of other departments to know about your land?

- Repeat for all lands.

- Transition: Vacate all but one land. All members step into that land except for members of that land. Be a good tourist in this land, so be respectful, curious, etc. Members of the "host" land listen as observers on the side. This is not interactive at this point.

- Phase 2: Interview questions for visitors to organizational lands (your land).

- What is it like to step into this department/land?

- What is important here?

- What are the challenges and pressures?

- What help or support do you need from other departments?

- Ask real land's citizens: What did they get right?

  - On a sticky note, or piece of paper, ask visitors to jot down one thing to remember about this land and leave this sticky note in that land.

- Repeat process for all lands.

- Transition: Once completed, lift the tape of all wedges and invite all into "our land," the space of shared experience and equity.

- Phase 3: Organizational our land questions (our land).

  - What is it like to be here with no departmental separation?

  - Having experienced all that has been shared and now standing together, what seems to be different for you now?

  - What is available from here?

  - Walk through all the sticky notes left by visitors and choose a few that you feel are important for your larger system to remember. Post those somewhere—on the board room table or a flip chart (or when working virtually: a Jamboard/Miro) page.

  - Invite everybody to sort those into themes

- Phase 4: Final action.

  - Examine the themes emerging from this activity and create workgroups or task forces to work on creating solutions for the emerging collective challenges. Throughout, leverage opportunities to expand a culture that thrives on diversity and inclusion!

Quotes from the interviews

"Revealing the system to itself, reading the emotional field, these now have become so ingrained in me."

- THE DIRECTOR OF TALENT MANAGEMENT
OF A MAJOR MULTINATIONAL

"I want to be able to help people to see things that they were unable to see. Because if you tell them: 'hey you need to do this and that,' they just give you that smile. But if you're able to ask them some questions or help them to see it from a different perspective, they even ask you for those practices eventually."

- BOARD MEMBER OF A SCRUM ORGANIZATION

2. Use the edge model as a lens to navigate change and facilitate emergence

In our training courses, we use Arnold Mindell's edge model as a powerful lens to track change processes and facilitate emergence (see picture on the next page). Basically, it is a pyramid shape where an edge divides the known and the unknown, the existing and the new, the present and the future, and the foreground and the background.

The edge separates who I identify myself to be from what I am becoming, or forced to become. For example, a shy person who needs to give a presentation to a big audience or someone who is expatriating to an unfamiliar country. It could also be what is already present but challenging to identify with. For example, someone who has made an embarrassing mistake or an LGBTQ person who does not dare to come out of the closet.

Individual Edge

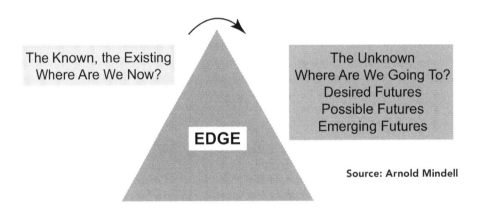

This model is about the growth curve of evolution. That also explains why it has infiltrated common language, making the statement that something "feels edgy" or that something is a big "edge" to accomplish. Edges are often not "chosen." They tend to "find us" within the growth curve of normal human evolution. It might show up in ways completely out of our control or our own making, hence the association with it being "edgy" or difficult. Death, pandemics, divorce, and the economy demanding layoffs are but a few of the difficult ones not necessarily chosen. Even positive changes, like getting married or being promoted, demands updating the resume and beginning to identify with the "new" you.

It is also present at the team and organizational level. There, it separates who we identify ourselves to be from what we are becoming, or forced to become. For example, a start-up turning into a scale-up, or a country team that is going global.

If an organization wants to digitalize, it moves from the existing business ("the known") to one that is digitalized ("the unknown"). To get there, many changes need to be made, or—in the language of the edge model—many edges need to be crossed. For example, it could be that the business model needs to be adjusted and that processes and structures need to be redesigned. And there may be tension in the organization as employees feel uncertain about their jobs and skills. All edges to be crossed...

And not only the team or organization have to cross these edges, but also individual members. A team or organization can only cross an edge until the majority of stakeholders are ready (see multiple edges picture below; please note that some individuals have crossed the edge already, while others have not).

Team Edge

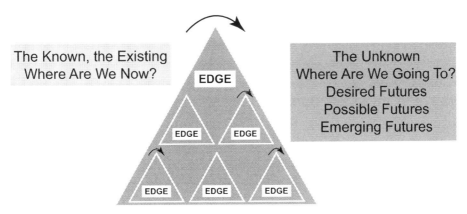

For a Systems Inspired Leader, it is not only important to support the whole system to cross an edge, but also to be aware of the individual edges. People do not cross edges at the same time. There are the early adopters, the early majority, the late majority, and the ones who may never cross the edge. As a leader, you must keep a close eye on all of them and be aware that change is an emotional journey that takes time. Systemic evolution includes and respects diversity.

Crossing edges is not only normal. It actually is the systemic evolution of us in our daily lives; we basically do it all the time. If you are working on your computer and suddenly your phone rings, your attention shifts from the computer to the phone. Crossing this edge is not very difficult and feels part of the natural flow of life.

From a Relationship Systems point of view, it becomes interesting to notice when a change (or possible change) feels "edgy" and not so comfortable. In these cases, the current identity of a relationship system is being challenged. For example, a traditional organization with a strong hierarchy that is forced by market pressures to become more agile and reduce the number of management layers is likely to be challenged in its identity. A transition or transformation is required from what the relationship system identified with (who they are) to what it did not identify with (who they are not). The more the new identity is unfamiliar, denied, or marginalized, the greater the edge to be crossed. A similar dynamic is happening when an advanced network organization is exploring its next phase of evolution or when systems are confronted with taboo topics (the "elephants in the room").

For Systems Inspired Leaders, it is key to recognize, name, and normalize these edges. They often get accompanied by non-verbal signals of discomfort, disturbances in the emotional field, and edge behaviors (see table on the page opposite for some examples). The system is getting out of its comfort zone and into a more stressful and potentially conflictual situation, often as a result of "reacting to" the discomfort.

Examples of Edge Behavior

- Nervous laughter

- Change in tone of voice

- Going blank

- Changing the topic

- Unfinished sentences and phrases

- Confusion

- Being frozen – "deer in the headlights"

- Fidgeting

- Uncomfortable silence

Revealing the system to itself becomes particularly vital in these instances. Useful questions are:

- What is it like?

- How do you feel?

- What is edgy here?

- What are we avoiding?

- What is holding us back?

- What needs to be addressed?

This is about reflecting on what is happening in the moment, noticing the edge behaviors and shifts in the emotional field. Being a narrator/commentator of what you see, hear, and sense happening rather than staying silent (remember, you are not watching TV!). Pressing the pause button will quiet the thinking mind as the voice of intuition is being accessed, exploring together what is trying to happen. These make the system aware of itself and allow it to evolve.

Something new is knocking at the door and asking to be welcomed. It's the birthplace of emergence, the place where learning deepens and growth flourishes. As the saying goes, "There is no learning in the comfort zone; there is no comfort in the learning zone."

There is also that sense of excitement and anticipation—however scary it may be—to enter this place of new life and possibility. Ultimately, we know it is about growing and manifesting our (collective) potential. And there is the trust that this "sitting in the fire" will bring something valuable and worthwhile, surrendering into the realization that we are all being held in this process, trusting that life will only give us those challenges that we are capable to navigate; that our life force is there with us. That it is just as curious to see if and how we are navigating the edge.

From a systemic point of view, it looks like the 3rd entity of the relationship system is instinctively adapting, "dreaming" up a new way of being, and looking for new qualities and roles to emerge so that it can find a new balance/identity. The individual parts must rearrange themselves (they need to "re-constellate") to give life to the expression of this new or expanded identity. Working this is true Relationship Systems Intelligence in action!

As we discussed in Chapter 3, we live in a world full of complex challenges, challenges without a technically "right" answer as the cause-and-effect relationships are too complex. Helping systems to cross, or at least explore, these edges will help to determine doable and intelligent ways forward in a complex world.

Looking at the pyramid, you will notice that the smallest edges (or distances to cross) are at the top of the pyramid. Here, the distance between the current identity and the new/expanded identity is at its shortest. This is what we call the minimum viable edge (MVE; a term coined by Leslie J. Morse, a specialist in the Agile/Scrum world) and constitutes the easier access point to change. The biggest edges (or distances to cross) are at the bottom of the pyramid. Crossing that "no man's" land signals a long and difficult journey.

Individual Edge

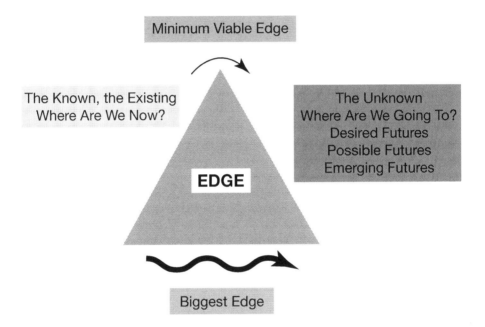

For example, if you want to run a marathon, it is easier to start your training with a short distance first rather than go for the full track. Or, if you want to digitalize your organization, it will be easier to first visit organizations that have already transitioned and ask them about their learnings rather than immediately designing a new organization. When change management fails, it is likely because the change was literally kicking the system across that vast space and making the change too big or sudden.

It is, therefore, important as a Systems Inspired Leader to become masterful at identifying, together with your team, the MVEs as ways to reduce the magnitude of change and ease the crossing of edges. This is what navigating change skillfully looks like!

Most organizations spend significant time developing their vision (their "to-be") and the strategic plan towards it, e.g., turn-over doubled, healthy product pipeline, going global, no carbon footprint, no safety incidents. Given that we live in a complex world, we know there is not a straight line to these visions. It is key to stay open for new possibilities and adapt to ongoing changes/disruptions (new technologies, new legislation, natural disasters), and determine intelligently the next vital step on the journey. Working with the edge model is a great asset here. It helps you, together with your team, to explore and connect with what is trying to happen in a complex and fast-changing world and develop viable ways to cross the emerging edges.

Practical applications

- When a staff member (or your team) describes an issue to you, draw the edge model in your mind's eye and ask yourself the following questions:

  - Where are they now?

  - Where do they want to go to?

  - What edge behaviors do I notice?

  - What could be a minimum viable edge (MVE) here?

- Or, you can introduce the team member to the edge model and explore the above together.

  For example, suppose someone says: "Decision making is too slow in this organization. We are bureaucratic, and I'm getting fed up with it and frustrated." Then, the picture could appear as follows:

Team Edge

Possible MVE: Discuss in
Next Team Meeting

Slow Decision
Making

Fast Decision
Making

Biggest Edge

The edge behavior displayed by this team member is frustration. Other edge behaviors could be irritation, confusion, blame, criticism.

- In a meeting, observe edge behaviors and reveal at least two of them during the meeting. Reflect afterward about the impact of these interventions.

- Ask the "miracle question" to your team to explore the pull of the desired state:

  - What if we had arrived at the place we are longing for, how does it look and feel? What's the weather/landscape like? How is it different from where we are now?

  - What is the dream/longing behind the complaint/ disappointment?

Quotes from the interviews

"[The edge model] is very important to me. I can see edge behavior in myself now and in the system; I did not look at it before."

- THE CEO OF A GLOBAL TRAINING ORGANIZATION

"If I do not go over the edge, the team won't get over the edge. So, it makes me push a bit forward."

- THE CEO OF AN EXECUTIVE AND SYSTEMS COACHING COMPANY

3. Monitor the ground conditions for change

For successful and sustainable change to happen, the following ground conditions must be fulfilled (source Margaret Wheatley). Revealing the system to itself plays an important role in all of them.

- New information must enter the system: who, what, where, when.

- There is a sense of shared purpose about the change: how is this going to be meaningful for me and us?

- All voices are invited to give input about how the change will occur. This activates the co-creative powers and taps the collective wisdom. Together, we discover how we will cross the edge.

- Everyone understands how input will be used and final decisions are made. This is not a commitment to implement all input, but to bring information from all parts of the system to the surface and in so doing, making more sustainable and creative decisions.

We know from experience that these conditions are often not met. Many organizations do not invest the time upfront to prepare well for the change, impacting particularly the last three bullet points. Reacting to the speed of change, rather than pausing and creating from it, often results in going fast initially but needing to re-do and actually slowing down the implementation. For example, think of the impact of an incomplete design, confusion, demoralization, resistance, sabotage. Go slow in order to go fast would have been much more effective and efficient. Like you hear often in organizations: *"We have no time and resources to do things right first time, but we always have time and resources to do rework."*

Frank remembers how some of his foreign colleagues were sometimes surprised by the role of staff councils in the Netherlands. Basically, they have a legal right to give advice about an intended reorganization, and in this way, they provide a structured way to listen to the voice of the employees. A "request for advice" must be submitted, detailing the case for change, the proposed changes, the implementation plan, and the impact on people. This process takes time and is, therefore, sometimes seen as a step that causes delay. But afterward, most acknowledged the advantages of this approach: the need to articulate clearly what the change is about, what the business case is, and how to deal with the implementation ensured that the plan was better thought through. And the subsequent conversation with the staff council made them aware of valid concerns and helpful suggestions from the employee's point of view, and in this way, it enriched plan and creating buy-in.

Practical application

- There are many ways to organize the collective input and arrange communications, depending on the scope and context of the change initiative. Some examples are focus groups, surveys, and town hall gatherings. The key point is to keep the ground conditions in mind when you navigate change. It is investing upfront to accelerate implementation at the back end. People are invested in the future they have helped to create.

- Think of a successful and unsuccessful change initiative (can be organizational or personal) and review them against the ground conditions for change. What are you learning about what constitutes sustainable change?

Quotes from the interviews

"Get all key stakeholders to design the change; when you give people a voice, even if they do not agree with the outcome, they will buy-in because they have been part of the process."

- THE CEO OF REGIONAL COACHING
AND TRAINING ORGANIZATION

"There is always change happening in an organization; it is a constant piece. There may be a clinical start and end day, but actually, change is happening all the time. Therefore, I think the ground conditions for change are so important. We need

to be clear that we are always collecting the voices of the

system. We need to know how they are processed, who does

what with them, and when we are going to give feedback on

who makes the final decision."

- A CUSTOMER OPERATIONS MANAGER

OF A MAJOR MULTINATIONAL

4. Be neutral when revealing the system to itself

Revealing the system to itself must be done in a neutral way, without judgment. You need to embrace everything that is present, knowing that all voices carry wisdom. This is a place where consciously holding Metaskills (e.g., Deep Democracy, respect, curiosity) will make a difference. Being judgmental (e.g., "Come on, this is not a very practical idea.") will shut the system down, enforce top-down leadership, and lead to the system missing out on vital information. Also appreciating the input from some people ("What a great idea!"), and not from others, will make people feel excluded and therefore not contributing to the full.

We acknowledge that this can be a challenging stance as a leader because you are also part of the system, and your voice is important and needs to be heard. It requires practice to do this skillfully. Knowing how to contribute while not using the rank of your role is an important consideration.

An interesting finding from the interviews was the ability of leaders to be explicit about the "hats" they wear. For example, be clear when speaking from the "colleague" hat, or from the "leader hat," or from the "out-of-the-box thinker" hat. One person did this even literally in an intern program she was facilitating. When she put up a little black hat with "CEO" on it, people knew she was now speaking from a different voice. It is a good practice to speak last from the "leader hat," letting others give their view first, so they are not adjusting their input based on your perspective. Also, present your views and ideas with a sense of humility, as input rather than as the ultimate truth.

Practical application: blank access questions

A good practice is to use blank access questions when you are revealing the system to itself and reading the emotional field. These questions support the emergence/unfolding process and help to bring new insight and awareness. They are called blank access questions because people can choose from which information channel they answer. Instead of forcing the channel, you may ask questions offering them multiple options like what they see, feel, hear, or think. What we know from experience is that they will choose the channel that they currently are in, and we can then work from there. These questions are your friends, as you can always use them, and when you are unsure what to ask next...☺

- How is this landing?

- What are you becoming aware of?

- What does it remind you of?

- What is it like?

- What is happening?

- What is trying to happen?

- How do you know you are having that experience (e.g., anxiety)?

- What is here now?

- What else?

- What is next?

- What is new now?

- What is a metaphor for this?

Quotes from the interviews

> "[At times] I am the facilitator, then I take off that hat and become the leader. I found myself pretty competent at this, and still, becoming a neutral leader is really difficult."
>
> - THE HR DIRECTOR OF A RETAIL ORGANIZATION

> "It is really hard not to judge in real life. But knowing that is not a justification to go there."
>
> - A DIRECTOR OF A HEALTH SERVICES AGENCY

> "I focus a lot on what is happening between people. I listen, listen, listen, and defer judgment. This also makes me a more pleasant person…"
>
> - AN OWNER OF A LOCAL COACHING COMPANY

5. Remember that change is an emotional journey

Revealing the system to itself helps the system to navigate change skillfully. And going through change is an emotional process. Sometimes it goes quick; sometimes it takes longer. Especially if the identity of a person is threatened, it takes time. For example, if a person loses their job or did not get the job or promotion they hoped for.

For leaders, it is important to realize that you are often ahead of the change curve. For example, suppose you already knew about a big reorganization or merger that had to be kept confidential. When the news finally breaks, you must be able to step into someone else's shoes and acknowledge that they may need time to accept the new reality and may not immediately be ready to look to the future.

A helpful tool is the change curve below. It is an adaption of the famous grief model of Elisabeth Kubler-Ross. Track where people are on this curve and help them to go through it. It is also helpful to educate your team about it, so people can help each other. The key is to meet people where they are on the change curve. Rational arguments do not typically work very well in the initial phases. The emotions must first be released and worked through. Also, use your coaching skills, as this is often more effective than giving advice.

The Change Curve

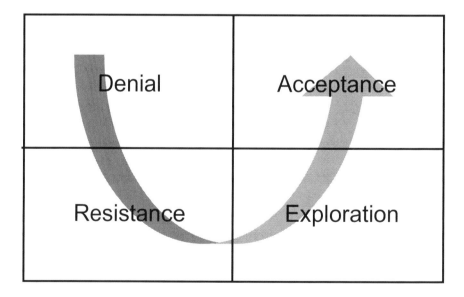

Adapted from Kubler-Ross

Practical application: helping people through the change curve

STAGE	POSSIBLE STRATEGIES
Denial: People do not believe that the change is going to happen. They think it will get "normal" again. They remain in the past.	• Reflect what you see, hear, and feel to the individual: "I get the sense that you do not believe this is going to happen." • Normalize: "I can fully understand that this is very different than you expected." (Stating this does NOT mean that you agree with them.) • Confirm: "The only thing I can say to you right now is that the change will go ahead. It will not go away." • Give time: "Take your time to process the news and let me know if you have any questions or whether you need my help."
Resistance: People become angry, frustrated, and anxious. There can also be despair and sadness. This stage is full of emotions.	• Reflect what you see, hear, and feel to the individual: "I notice that you seem to have strong emotions about this." • Normalize: "I can fully understand this. It is quite normal to experience this in your situation" (Stating this does NOT mean that you agree with them.) • Help to express the emotions (so-called "ventilation"): "What are you feeling right now?" "What's it like?" • Acknowledge the feelings: "I notice that you are sad," and continue ventilating: "What are you feeling now?" "What is there now?"

STAGE	POSSIBLE STRATEGIES
Resistance continued...	• Help to leave the past behind and to let go: "What needs to be grieved/ acknowledged about the past that will not be there anymore?" "What will you not miss anymore?" • If the person is ready for it, start discussing the new reality and what it means for them.
Exploration: The new reality has sunk in, and people are ready to face the future and explore what is possible for them.	• Reflect what you see, hear, and feel: "I notice that you are more open right now to look at the future." • Normalize: "I can fully understand that it is not so clear yet where you want to go." • Explore possibilities: "What would be possible for you from here?" • As appropriate, amplify this: "If this actually was an important opportunity and crossroad in your life, what would it be?"
Acceptance: People have found new meaning. They are ready to move forward and take on the new challenge.	• Reflect back what you see, hear, and feel: "I notice that you have regained your energy and enthusiasm." • Offer support: "Is there anything I can to do to help?" • Champion them: "I believe you can do this."

Quote from the interviews

"It is about taking people on an emotional journey. If you provide an environment where you can help people through their emotions or to verbalize their emotions or speak to their emotions, you can help them deal with change more effectively. And the tools gave me a vehicle to be able to facilitate those deeper conversations."

- THE CEO OF REGIONAL COACHING
AND TRAINING ORGANIZATION

ASSESS YOURSELF ON THIS COMPETENCY

- Rate yourself on a scale from 1 to 5 on the following beliefs and behaviors, where 1 means "I never do this," 3 means "I do this regularly," and 5 means "I do this all the time." [You can also use the digital assessment mentioned on the bonus page at the end of this book.]

- Add up the scores and determine how strong you are in this competency:

  - Between 10-20: you are becoming aware of this competency.

  - Between 20-30: you are developing skills in this competency.

  - Between 30-40: you are skilled in this competency.

  - Between 40-50: you are masterful in this competency.

- Now, determine what you would like to work on, using the ideas and practices of this chapter as input.

1. I regularly review performance data with my team to create insight and learning.	....
2. I actively work with the team on emergence and change rather than impose change top-down.	....

3. I actively track and sense what is happening in the moment and reflect this to my team to enhance self-awareness.	....
4. I use tools and techniques (e.g., constellations, designing the team alliance, polling) to reveal the system to itself.	....
5. I value diversity of input and encourage out-of-the-box thinking.	....
6. I actively use the edge model to track where we are in change processes.	....
7. I see edge behaviors as indicators of what is trying to happen in a system.	....
8. I regularly review whether the ground conditions for change are met for our change initiatives.	....
9. I offer my point of view in a way that invites further dialog.	....
10. I actively support my team on their emotional journey through change and invite them to do the same with the team.	....

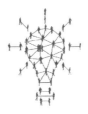

CHAPTER 8

DOING – WORKING WITH CONFLICT TO FACILITATE EMERGENCE

"I expect differences, I expect disagreement, and I expect conflict. And that is huge for me because I used to be scared of it. I'm still scared of it, actually. Now, I expect them. I know it is not a terrible thing. It is actually a good thing. So, that is another huge benefit to my leadership."

- THE OWNER OF A REGIONAL EXECUTIVE AND TEAM COACHING COMPANY

Definition of "Working with Conflict to Facilitate Emergence"

The ability to view and work with conflict as a systemic event and a signal that change is needed and something new is trying to emerge, shifting the perspective from, "Who is doing what to whom?" to "What is trying to happen?"

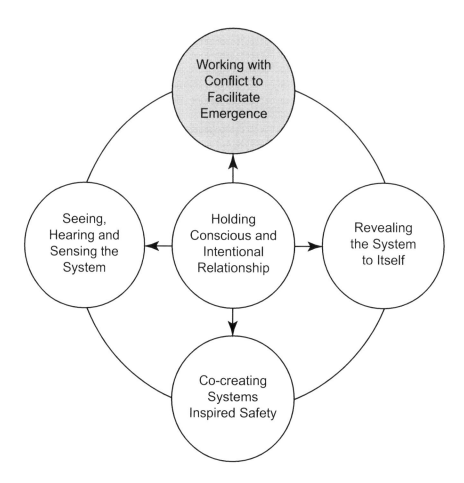

Link with Relationship Systems Intelligence (RSI)

While acknowledging that the RSI principles are interdependent and interconnected, the following principles link particularly well with this competency:

- Every member of a relationship system is a "voice of the system."

- Relationship systems rely on roles for their organization and execution of functions. Roles belong to the system, not only to the individuals that inhabit the system. Unproductive conflict is often caused by rigid polarization and a lack of role fluidity in the system.

- Relationship systems are in a constant state of emergence, always in the process of expressing their potential.

Ways to grow this competency

In this chapter, we discuss five powerful ways to help you advance this competency:

1. Hold conflict as a signal for emerging change.

2. Co-create Systems Inspired Safety (see also Chapter 9).

3. Honor the stages of successful conflict resolution.

4. Decrease negativity during conflict.

5. Create clarity upfront on how decisions are made

1. Hold conflict as a signal for emerging change

The word conflict often evokes negative reactions. It is not uncommon for people to describe themselves as "conflict-averse." There is the fear that it could damage the team spirit, cause hurt and separation, and can even lead to somebody being fired. While we acknowledge that this can happen, we hold conflict as something valuable and a key area to be worked on and revealed. We see it not only as an indicator that change is needed, but it also provides the map for it. In edge model language (see Chapter 7), you can say that during conflict, the system is at an edge and that new possibilities and futures want to emerge. Like someone said in the interviews, *"If there is conflict, you are close to something new; you are on the edge. So, it is actually a hopeful sign that you are not far away from something new to be born."*

The challenge, therefore, is to deal with conflict skillfully and create "productive conflict" (often also referred to as courageous conversations or generative dialogs). It is about turning conflict into rich, generative conversations. For this to happen, it is helpful to realize that the conflict or tension, while being present between individuals and experienced as personal, is also a systemic event. It is personal, and it belongs to the system. How, and where else, does this unease and strain show up on the team or in the system?

The classic example is when budget cuts must be implemented. This can create significant tension between individuals and departments. This tension is not only personal but also systemic. And by expressing it, it becomes a voice for the larger system's experience. As mentioned above, the key question shifts to "What is trying to happen?" rather than "Who did what to whom?" Normalizing these tensions and creating courageous, productive conversations and protocols for managing such conversations are some of the most important ways to co-create Systems Inspired Safety and leverage the collective wisdom (see also Chapter 9).

This is also why diversity within a team is so important. It brings a broad range of views and experiences to the table, creating valuable input for the way forward. Research indicates that effective solutions do not *only* require experts. Team members with less knowledge of the subject bring fresh eyes and questions, leading to critical re-examination and prototyping new and different ways.

Practical applications

- Choose or adjust your Metaskills (ref Chapter 6) to normalize conflict as a signal for change. Good examples for this might be being curious, trusting the system, non-attachment, and respect.

- Educate your team on the usefulness of conflict as a signal for change and normalize conflict as part of change and evolution. Examples of language for this might be: "Conflicts in teams are normal. They are signals for change, and they indicate that something new wants to emerge. They point us to the need to innovate." This softens the emotional field and creates openness for exploration.

- Ask your team: "What is trying to happen?" This shifts the focus away from the people to the relationship system.

- A creative, albeit provocative, way to think of conflict is that it is actually an unopened package of information that is being thrown around the room. Recognizing it as such is often a good metaphor for slowing down and getting curious about what is wrapped up in that package—other than the label it was given. (See also example on page 83.)

- In case of a very hot disagreement, ask somebody to help facilitate the conversation. Even the best of us cannot create positive outcomes from hot conflicts while a shouting match is happening!

Quote from the interviews

"I don't think anybody is ever comfortable in conflict, but I am more comfortable now. I know that not having conflict is more dangerous than having conflict, as long as it's managed well."

- A DIRECTOR OF A HEALTH SERVICES AGENCY

2. Co-create Systems Inspired Safety (see Chapter 9)

Co-creating Systems Inspired Safety is a vital condition for dealing with conflict effectively. It basically creates the space for people to speak up and engage in difficult and courageous conversations. Given its pivotal importance, we have devoted Chapter 9 to it.

3. Honor the stages of successful conflict resolution

Ideally, a conflict is constructive and serves the system well by creating new insight and change. However, conflict can also become unproductive, especially when it polarizes the system and emotions start running high. When a conflict gets really hot, it is useful to apply the basic principles and techniques of mediation. Provided sufficiently trained, this can be done by the Systems Inspired Leader or team members themselves. If not, reach out to an outside facilitator.

The first step is to pause the escalation of blame, frustration, and criticism. Breaking up the interactive blaming is the start, as otherwise, it is simply going to escalate further. Set the stage where they take turns to face you as they speak their frustration. This is what is known as "ventilation," a powerful technique originating from mediation and alternative dispute resolution practices, and an important skillset to educate the team around. This is not an interactive process between them, but rather allowing them to let off steam. Do this in small sound bites, one person after the other, making sure all have equal time. This is critical because continued frustration and anger interactively expressed can create a negative spiral of blame and defensiveness. The conversation will simply escalate into more toxicity, polarization, and exhaustion in the system. By letting off steam in a non-interactive way, the emotional field can calm down and soften and open a space for a productive conversation. In big groups, it can be advisable to take a break in silence after this process to breathe and rest. It is important, then, for them to take time for themselves rather than talking to each other. When they come back, test the emotional field and see whether more ventilation needs to take place.

Throughout the process of ventilation, it is critical to listen for interests in common—even if it is in a statement that the experience is very difficult. That is something they can agree on. Find these nuggets and repeat those to them. **This is the start of alignment.** As the emotional field softens, alignment can begin to be shaped from these common interests. For example, if there is a hot conflict about divesting a part of the business, explore the common ground.

Key questions to get there:

- "Why is it important to resolve this?"

- "Are you (we) willing to resolve this without blame?"

- "What is it that you notice as aspects of agreement?"

It is important to differentiate between alignment and agreement. Alignment is looking for the common goal, purpose, vision, or strategy ("looking in the same direction"), agreement is landing a concrete solution or way forward together ("shaking hands"). Take, for example, a conflict between two people on how they run a project together. One feels that the other does not contribute enough and misses critical deadlines. The other does not feel understood as they are juggling other important projects. Creating alignment here could be that they both want this project to be successful, and the agreement could be to develop a realistic delivery plan, with an early warning system if deadlines cannot be met. The key for alignment is that the parties involved are looking in the same direction; they are side by side. To literally put the issue in front can serve as a useful instrument for this (see also below on "practical applications").

The final step is to **problem solve and come to an agreement.** This involves well-known techniques like brainstorming, identifying pros and cons, and creating concrete and specific action steps. Throughout this process, read the emotional field actively, whatever it is and without interpretation. (For example, "I sense there is quite some tension in the room," or "it feels like the sun is coming through.") Grasp any opportunity to acknowledge the partnership/team when things improve. ("I appreciate there is more listening to each other now," or "I appreciate your willingness to start solving this together.") The skill of "fading" is important too: when things go well, let the partnership/team work through the issue without interruption. When the conflict flares up again, step in and reveal it. If needed, start another ventilation round and ensure that they speak to you rather than to each other.

In the interviews, a powerful example of creating alignment surfaced. There was a conflict about managing a youth center between a health services agency and an important stakeholder and their elected official. The agency wanted a more co-creative and adaptive approach, and the elected preferred a more law enforcement way.

"Traditionally public health and law enforcement don't get along; they are completely different systems. Therefore, for several years, there was an ongoing conflict that grew to a point where the relationship completely blew up; we could not even be in the same room together. In addition, exactly when I took on my director role, we were told by our elected official that we had to figure out a way to get along. It was an incredibly difficult task. My team and I really understood that if we were going to work with them, we had to understand law enforcement. So, we created meetings, with a neutral facilitator, to help us come together and listen to each other. We began by having conversations about what we hoped for the youth center and why it would be good if we were able to work together. We had a dinner together where it was really about seeing the humanity in each of us. My team is relationship systems trained and we decided not to privilege our perspective. And gradually, we started to understand each other better. I learned, for example, that when they make an arrest, there are very strict legal mandates to ensure their own safety, as their lives are constantly at risk. That explained their focus on strict mandates while we favor a more flexible approach. We learned to understand what they needed and they started to understand what was non-negotiable for us. In the end, we were able to find ways to fit our perspectives together. And fourteen months later, they're probably our strongest partner. We have great conversations, we know we come from different perspectives, and we know we don't always see eye to eye. I don't think we could have done this without the relationship systems skills and tools. The relationship systems lens was totally instrumental in making this work."

Practical application: putting the issue out in front

When the partnership/team is getting aligned and ready to problem-solve, it can be helpful to take an object representing the issue ((could be a pen, a bottle, a marker, a flip chart paper) and put it in front. When there is conflict, the issue lives between the partnership/team. It's what separates them (see the first picture below). From this place of separation, it is very hard to solve it together. Ask the partnership/team to literally put the object in front, making it a collective and embodied experience (see the second picture below). Then explore what it is like to see the issue in front and how it is different than before. This is a tangible and powerful way to take the issue out of the relationship and start working on it together. It often even helps to define the issue more clearly.

Marita remembers her surprise when she arrived for a coaching session with a board that pulled out a plastic bagel as the object to put in front during an alignment conversation. It was a heritage of the actual bagel from the refreshment table when she first introduced them to this concept of putting the problem out in front!

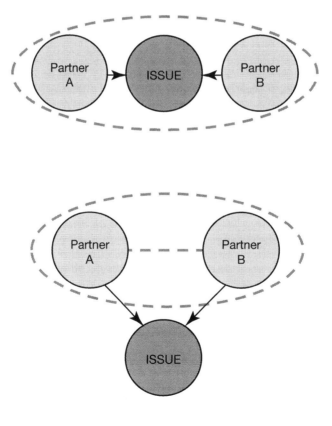

Quotes from the interviews

"From a conflict management perspective, I do alignment practically daily. I ask a lot: 'Why is it important to resolve it? Why do we have to resolve this? What is the bigger picture?'"

- THE CHIEF OPERATING OFFICER OF A TRIBUNAL

"Collaboration always comes when you begin to have people with different goals come together to work towards one bigger vision."

- THE CEO OF A GLOBAL COACH TRAINING
AND CONSULTING COMPANY

4. Decrease negativity during conflicts

Conflict can create negativity and toxicity and, as a result, impact team efficacy. The Systems Inspired Leader monitors this carefully, reveals it, and takes measures—together with the team—to make the conflict productive again.

It is useful to build on the work of John Gottman here. He researched what constituted successful marriages and found four behaviors that cause toxicity and predict divorce. He called them the "four horsemen of the Apocalypse": blaming (criticizing), defensiveness, stonewalling, and contempt. These toxins reinforce each other: one evokes the other, and together they create a negative spiral. Gottman's findings are equally relevant to the organizational context. Also, here toxins play up frequently and create its damaging impact on morale and collaboration. Toxins reflect unskillful communication. The underlying intention is to make things better but the way it is delivered is ineffective. Here are some ways to work with it:

- Educate your team on the toxins and create a conflict protocol together (see below for a practical way to do this).

- Reveal the toxins (e.g., "I notice there is judgment here") and their impact ("it is making the conflict toxic and therefore less effective"). If appropriate, normalize and/or set up ventilation as discussed above.

- Choose powerful Metaskills (ref Chapter 6): for example, curiosity, positivity, open to influence, and humor/lightness.

- Refer to the team alliance (ref Chapter 6) as a reminder of how to be together when things get difficult.

- When there is a lot of complaining, allow for some of it to be spoken, and then begin to look for the hope or dream behind the complaint. Ask people what they would like instead, amplify this with image and story weaving, and explore how to get there.

- Train your team to use I-language rather than you-language. For example: "I don't feel heard right now" sounds very different from "You are such bad listeners." And, of course, tone of voice and non-verbals are also important here.

- Use a "soft start-up" when addressing an issue. For example: "We had an awkward moment in the meeting just now. Could we talk about that?" This is very different from a "hard start-up": "You were very rude to me in the meeting. This is unacceptable." In the soft start-up, there is no attack or defense; you neutrally present the issue.

If people do not feel that their voice is listened to, they will become resistant. Resistance can take many shapes. The resistance line on the next page is a great indicator of the escalating levels of resistance. What to monitor first is covert resistance: the repeated jokes in meetings, the sarcastic jokes at the coffee machine, the excuses when things haven't been followed up, and the gossip. If you miss these signals, the conflict can quickly get polarized and become unproductive, even resulting in strikes and withdrawals. When there is polarization in a relationship system, people take fixed positions on a topic. In systems terms, people identify with their roles/voices and lack role fluidity. They forget that the roles/voices belong to the system, not to the individuals. A Systems Inspired Leader monitors these dynamics carefully. They know that if this is not addressed at an early stage, the costs (of not working well together) are enormous.

The Resistance Line

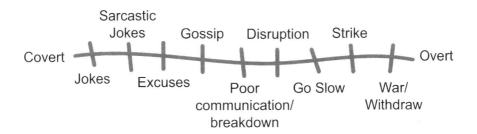

Source: Myrna Lewis

Practical application: walking the toxin grid

To educate your team on toxins, you can walk the toxin grid.

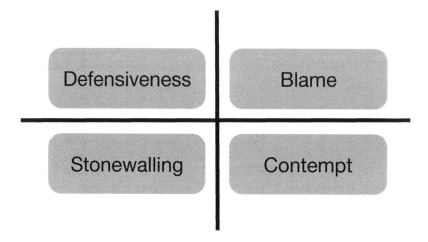

Create a grid on the floor with the four toxins and let the team connect with each of them.

- Ask them to share some examples of what each toxin looks like in real life to anchor the concepts (see the table opposite).

- Then, ask the people to step into the square that they think is most commonly occupied by the team. Notice how people are distributed; normally, there are different points of view. Ask what situations bring that toxin out in the team.

- Then ask: how is that toxin trying to be helpful? What is the belief behind it?

- Ask each team member to go to the one they individually most often employ. What situations bring it out in them? (This step helps to normalize the toxins: we all use them from time to time.)

- Review the antidotes to the team toxins (see table opposite).

- Have the team develop a conflict protocol (see **Appendix 4**).

TOXIN	BEHAVIORS
Blaming/Criticism	Finger-pointing, aggressive attacking, bullying, dominating, overly driving, harsh start-up (immediately starting with negative and accusatory behavior)
Defensiveness	Saying it's not their fault, refusal to take responsibility, victimizing, not open to influence.
Stonewalling	Disengagement, passivity, not open to influence, avoidance, withdrawal, going around the chain of command
Contempt	Personal attacks, sarcasm, hostile humor, eye-rolling, demeaning gossip, disrespectful tone, undermining.

TOXIN	POSSIBLE ANTIDOTES
Blaming/Criticism	Skillful feedback (e.g., situation, behavior, impact, request) Feed forward (tips/advice for next time) Soft start-up (first connect, then raise the issue) Genuine curiosity Use I-language rather than you-language
Defensiveness	Genuine curiosity 2 percent truth (If some of it were true, what could it be?)

Stonewalling	You are a voice of the system—speak up! Transparency Get mediation
Contempt	Skillful feedback (situation, behavior, impact, request) Practice respectful communication Personal development (as contempt is also toxic for yourself, it makes you sick)

Quotes from the interviews

"I was forty when the relationship systems approach came into my life, and I honestly didn't know that we could be so nice to each other and that humans could be so respectful. That was probably the biggest revolution for me as a human. I started to look inside and look at my own toxins. What toxins do I bring to the table? How am I toxic in my relationships and even in my teams?"

- A CEO OF REGIONAL COACHING AND
TRAINING ORGANIZATION

"I don't allow toxic communication. When it is there, I name it. When there is a rumor about other employees in the company, I just stop it. And I say that this is contagious and it is not part of our values as an organization."

- THE REGIONAL HR DIRECTOR OF A GLOBAL TRADING COMPANY

5. Create clarity upfront on how input will be used and decisions are made

While Systems Inspired Leaders create from the system and facilitate emergence, this does not mean that they do not make decisions themselves anymore—you can, and sometimes you should, according to the manual of authorities. The key difference is that you have worked with your team/stakeholders extensively to tap the collective wisdom and establish what is wanting to happen. It can also be that a decision is taken higher up in the organization, and you and your team can only provide input. As we outlined in Chapter 7, when we discussed the ground conditions for change, it is important to create clarity upfront on how input will be used and how decisions are made.

Decisions can be taken in many ways depending on the circumstances. Here are some common approaches:

- The leader decides based on everyone's input.

- The majority vote (best to go for at least 70 percent). Tip: ask the remainder what they need in order to embrace this decision and see whether you can incorporate their needs/ideas. In this way, you use the wisdom of the minority.

- By consent (everyone can live with it, no one disagrees/vetoes).

- By consensus (everyone agrees).

Also, pay attention to how the decision is communicated. If needed, acknowledge that not everyone's preferred choice has been chosen and give a short rationale for this. If people know that their voice has been heard and considered, they will be much less resistant.

Quotes from the interviews

"I want to hear what we all have to say. And then the final decision lies with me. So being clear and direct is the way I deal with it."

- AN ASSOCIATE DIRECTOR OF A
HEALTH SERVICES AGENCY

"As much as we can we make decisions as a system. But sometimes, strategically, I may take a decision on my own but I'm very clear about that."

- THE CEO OF REGIONAL COACHING AND
TRAINING ORGANIZATION

ASSESS YOURSELF ON THIS COMPETENCY

- Rate yourself on a scale from 1 to 5 on the following beliefs and behaviors, where 1 means "I never do this," 3 means "I do this regularly," and 5 means "I do this all the time." [You can also use the digital assessment mentioned on the bonus page at the end of this book.]

- Add up the scores and determine how strong you are in this competency:

  - Between 10-20: you are becoming aware of this competency.

  - Between 20-30: you are developing skills in this competency.

  - Between 30-40: you are skilled in this competency.

  - Between 40-50: you are masterful in this competency.

- Now, determine what you would like to work on, using the ideas and practices of this chapter as input.

1. I see conflict as a signal that something new is trying to emerge.	....
2. I educate my team that conflict is normal, healthy, and the engine for change.	....

3. I actively invite different points of view to bring new and different information to the surface.	....
4. I see resistance/sabotage/revenge as signs that voices have not been heard sufficiently.	....
5. I actively allow the system to ventilate when emotions are running high and aim to de-escalate.	....
6. During conflicts, I actively look for common goals/ interests and seek alignment, and I expect the same from my team.	....
7. I recognize when a conflict becomes toxic and work this with my team.	....
8. When things get difficult, I refer to our team alliance and conflict protocol.	....
9. I see polarization (taking fixed positions on a topic) as a signal that the conflict is not productive anymore and an intervention is needed.	....
10. When difficult decisions must be made, we are clear as a team how input will be used and how decisions are made.	....

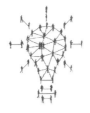

CHAPTER 9

DOING – CO-CREATING SYSTEMS INSPIRED SAFETY

"Safety is key and take what you can. It's not always going to be 100 percent safe. Lean into the relative percentage of safety, and build from there. And name it, honor it, and nurture it."

- THE FOUNDER AND CEO OF A REGIONAL COACHING AND TRAINING COMPANY

Definition of "Co-creating Systems Inspired Safety"

The ability to co-create a space where people feel comfortable to speak their truth and share their vulnerabilities, the ability to hold and open up a creative space. It lives in a Systems Inspired Culture where team members believe they will not be punished or humiliated for speaking up with ideas, questions, challenges, or mistakes.

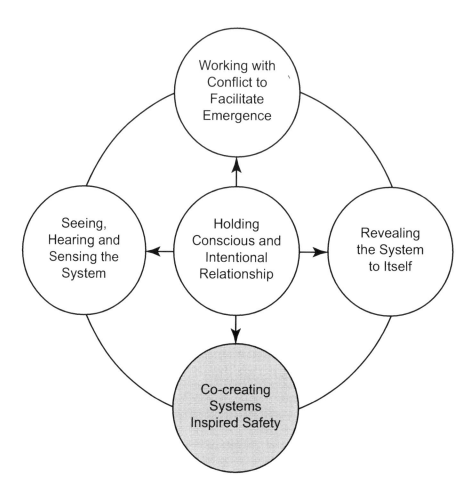

Link with Relationship Systems Intelligence (RSI)

While acknowledging that the RSI principles are interdependent and interconnected, the following principles link particularly well with this competency:

- Each relationship system has its own unique identity and "personality."

- Relationship systems are naturally intelligent, generative, and creative.

Ways to grow this competency

In this chapter, we discuss five powerful ways to help you advance this competency:

> 1. Consider Systems Inspired Safety as the foundation for people, teams, and organizations to flourish.
>
> 2. Leverage Systems Inspired Safety to create productive conflicts and emergence.
>
> 3. Honor and normalize that it takes time and effort to build Systems Inspired Safety.
>
> 4. Amp up positivity.
>
> 5. Be aware of your special position as a leader

1. Consider Systems Inspired Safety as the foundation for people, teams, and organizations to flourish.

Systems Inspired Safety is about intentionally co-creating the systemic conditions for people to speak up and share their truths. This is pivotal in a world faced with issues that are too complex to be solved by a single person, team, or organization. Systems Inspired Safety is closely linked to the concept of "psychological safety." This term was coined by Harvard Business School professor Amy Edmondson and refers to the belief that one will not be punished or humiliated for speaking up with ideas, questions, concerns, or mistakes. Edmondson promotes a "fearless organization" that enables learning, innovation, and growth. For her, it is the key to great teamwork. This was also the finding of the well-known Google study in 2012 (Project Aristotle), where psychological safety surfaced as the key ingredient for successful teams. It trumped (by far!) elements like skill diversity, backgrounds, friendships, and IQ levels.

Systems Inspired Safety emphasizes that this psychological safety is created from—and by—the relationship system itself. It is the responsibility and co-creation of everyone in the team/system. The key role of the Systems Inspired Leader is to invite, nurture, and empower it. Systems Inspired Safety allows people to be truly human, to step into their purpose, to share and live their dreams, and show their vulnerability and mistakes. It enables people to embrace their true selves and become the best they can be, not afraid to express what they stand for. It creates a strong sense of belonging and a feeling of a secure base/home, regardless of differences in style, opinions, rank, and privileges, and it prioritizes human relationships.

Deloitte highlighted in their 2020 Global Human Capital Trends Survey that "belonging," along with "well-being", is at the top of the Global Human Capital issues. According to the survey, 79 percent of respondents said that fostering a sense of belonging in the workforce was important to their organization's success in the next twelve to eighteen months, and 93 percent agreed that a sense of belonging drives organizational performance. And this lack of sense of belonging was reinforced by the COVID-19 pandemic where most people were forced to work from home, lost their daily passing contact, and could only make contact and build relationships digitally.

From a neuroscience perspective, we are wired to connect *and* to survive. For example, for a baby to survive, the ability to connect is its most important quality. If our sense of belonging is threatened, it is seen as an existential threat and makes us reactive, prompting a fight or flight response. The fear of rejection within a group, team, or organization could mean that we prefer to stay silent and conform, rather than speak up. We do not want to be seen as ignorant, incompetent, intrusive, or negative and become excluded as a result. Ask yourself how many times this week or month you stopped yourself from saying something difficult? When did you hit an edge to express what you really thought and felt? Fear shuts down our prefrontal cortex and narrows our creative, reasoning, and problem-solving capabilities. All this carries a high cost in a world that needs us to constantly come up with new and creative ideas and to speak up before things go wrong.

The Challenger accident in 1986 is a well-known example of what can happen when the confidence to speak truth to power is not present. In this accident, a space shuttle exploded a little more than a minute after lift-off and instantly killed the seven-person crew. The disaster was caused by leaking seals that were not designed to handle the unusually cold conditions of this launch. The risk of this happening was long known but never discussed as this felt too unsafe.

The challenge for teams and organizations, therefore, is to create a workplace in which people speak up rather than stay silent, challenge rather than conform, take initiatives rather than react, and know it's okay to fail rather than avoid taking the risk.

At the same time, we realize that a fully safe place may not exist in organizations. There may always be a residual fear of losing your job, damaging your career prospects, or exposing your performance rating and pay. The challenge then becomes to create a place that is safe enough to be courageous and vulnerable.

Practical application

Write a taboo subject or undiscussable topic in capital letters (to ensure anonymity) on a piece of paper and put it in a box. Someone on the team draws one and presents it passionately to the rest of the team, as input for a courageous conversation.

Quotes from the interviews

"So, how do I build psychological safety so that you can challenge me and it is not going to be detrimental to your career or any of that stuff?"

- THE DIRECTOR OF TALENT MANAGEMENT
OF A MAJOR MULTINATIONAL

"How safe do you want it to be and how far are you from that? And paradoxically, how safe is it to actually answer that question honestly? Usually, you want to find out what's the cost of not talking, because there's a price systems pay for not being safe."

- THE FOUNDER AND CEO OF A REGIONAL
COACHING AND TRAINING COMPANY

2. Leverage Systems Inspired Safety to create productive conflict and emergence

As indicated in the previous chapter, Systems Inspired Safety is a key requirement for having productive conflict and creating from the system. It is therefore not about creating a cozy place where everyone is in their comfort zone. On the contrary, it stretches you into what Amy Edmondson calls "the learning zone." Systems Inspired Safety helps to create a space where people speak their truth, where diversity is fully leveraged, and where productive conflict can flourish. It enables the information to flow freely and unlocks creativity and collective wisdom. It creates a space for generative dialog and magic, a space where something can emerge that no one could produce on their own.

At the same time, having successful courageous conversations and normalizing conflict as a signal for constructive change will grow Systems Inspired Safety. It is a self-reinforcing loop. It helps to continuously grow as a team, shifting the inquiry from, "Who is doing what to whom?" to "What is trying to happen?"

Practical application

Ask the "what if" question: When dealing with an important topic, ask every team member to reflect on what would be possible or available when all constraints/barriers were removed? What would the dream look like? Ask them to draw a picture of it or find a metaphor. Share the stories in a gallery tour and build the way forward from there.

Quotes from the interviews

"I think that standing for your beliefs a hundred percent and being able to have really good, passionate fights, and notice where you are triggered and notice how you recover, is all really good work."

- THE FOUNDER AND CEO OF A REGIONAL COACHING AND TRAINING COMPANY

"It is often helpful as the most senior leader to say: 'I'm feeling anxious about these things. Who else is feeling like that?' And let that be the topic of conversation."

- A CUSTOMER OPERATIONS MANAGER OF A MAJOR MULTINATIONAL

3. Honor and normalize that it takes time and effort to build Systems Inspired Safety

Building Systems Inspired Safety takes time, and it is easily destroyed. A Dutch saying goes, "It comes by foot and goes by horse." People need to experience that it is safe to speak up and show their vulnerability. Can you fall backward and trust that your colleagues will catch you? Systems Inspired Safety is not an end state nor a place of arrival. It needs to be created moment by moment.

Here are some ideas to build Systems Inspired Safety:

It starts with **building relationships, connecting, showing interest, knowing people's aspirations and dreams, and having a sense of their personal life** (e.g., whether they have a partner and/or children, how their parents are doing, what hobbies they have, or what challenges they face). It is seeing people as human beings rather than as resources to get the job done. Having coffee and lunch together are great ways to establish this—company dinners and outings, with and without partners, as well. A more advanced way is to organize "hero dinners" for your team. Each team member tells a story of how he or she has overcome a life challenge. This could be a major loss, a broken dream, a threatening illness, a career switch, a move to a new country, etc. At the end of each story, a piece of music is played, chosen by the storyteller, to deepen the connection between the story and the storyteller. It is key that the first storyteller sets the tone by telling a truly personal story. That could be you as a Systems Inspired Leader.

Designing the team alliance (see Chapter 6) is a powerful way to co-create Systems Inspired Safety. This is about defining how you will flourish together and what you will do when things get difficult. It creates consciousness and intentionality.

Sharing your vulnerability as a leader and wearing your "colleague hat" is very powerful. You are being a role model and giving permission to your team members to do the same. It is okay to say that you do not know, and it can be motivating/inspiring for your team to hear you say that you are confident that this team can find the answer.

Reframing "mistakes" and "failures" as information to create the next prototype is not only critical for building safety, but also for creating a sense of belonging by being part of the solution. Every time there is an experience of "failure," it will provide the scaffolding of how to improve and improvise better. Encouraging people to experiment, try things out, and learn and come back with new insights are simple ways to encourage innovation. We know that this can be quite challenging in high-pressure and stressful situations. At the same time, it's the ideal playground to learn as a team or organization to create from the situation instead of only reacting to it. Take the COVID-19 crisis as an example. Becoming skillful here will save a lot of time and damage.

Reading the emotional field to sense whether it is safe enough for people to speak up and work with that. Discover what makes it difficult, brainstorm what will make it easier, and then create co-responsibility for making it happen.

Be mindful when to speak. The timing of *when* you say things can be an important factor in creating Systems Inspired Safety. As a general rule, go first when showing vulnerability or courage (e.g., admitting a mistake, or committing to something edgy) and go last when exploring a new topic or a sensitive issue (to avoid that your perspective will shut down certain voices). Joseph Jaworski, a renowned leadership scholar, applies three golden rules for creating generative dialog:

1. Ask yourself if it's your "turn" to speak (tune in to the system).

2. Ask yourself if you have truly listened.

3. Ask yourself what you want to contribute in service of the whole.

Holding space by being fully present with whatever comes up. Being open, neutral, and non-judgmental are key skills of a Systems Inspired Leader, requiring significant self-knowledge and mastery of own triggers. See also Chapter 7.

Practical application: Leveraging the practice of "yes and..."

As the pace of change continues to increase, many leaders are now looking to the theater world to help them to develop what is known as an improviser mindset. Adopting an improviser mindset can help leaders to dance in the moment and co-create from unexpected emergence.

If you have ever been to an improvisation show, you will know that the worst improvisers block. For example, one performer makes an "offer," pretending a cushion is a "fluffy cat" and then another performer blocks them: "That's not a cat, that's a cushion." Improvisation over! What great improvisers do is listen to and build on offers, using a general rule from improvisational comedy, "yes and…" So, returning to our example, improviser two could instead offer up: "Yes, and that cat is so furry it's going to set off my allergies! *Sneeze*"

The "yes and…" principle is also an incredibly useful tool for the Systems Inspired Leader. Let's say a new hire is asking to book a vacation at a particularly busy time for your team. As opposed to blocking their offer with an outright "no," you could instead build on their offer with a "yes and…" "Yes, it's great to hear you're booking in vacation early, and I wonder whether we can look at other times in our diaries as that happens to be one of the busiest weeks of the year for this team."

Now you have opened up a dialog as opposed to shutting down the conversation. Of course "yes and…" is much more than language: it's an attitude! For example, if you replied in the same example with, "Yes and that's a stupid idea!" that would still be a block. Despite the "yes and…" language, your attitude—and probably your body language—would be clearly saying "no!"

We encourage you to think of ways you can bring the attitude of "yes and…" to the offers in your life. Try it with your colleagues, your partner, your children, and notice how it opens up the conversation as opposed to closing it down. Meet the person where they are, show them you have received their offer, and then propose a build. And once you get comfortable, get creative with your language (and body language) in order to embrace more of a "yes and…" attitude. You could try leaning in, echoing their language, and using other phrases like, "yes, so…" This simple technique will help you to lead with an improviser mindset and collaborate in a much more present, connected, and creative way.

Practical application: check-in and check-out

The **check-in and check-out** are important and often forgotten elements in a meeting and a great way to co-create Systems Inspired Safety. In essence, they allow the Systems Inspired Leader to meet the system where it is—not where you, as leader, thought it was or you want it to be.

The prime purpose of the **check-in** to gather all voices in the room and get people present for the meeting. Many leaders have a tendency to immediately dive into the content of a meeting, in order not to lose time. But if people are not present, this will boomerang. The check-in provides an open space at the start of a meeting for people to say what is on their minds. It could be they had a difficult meeting beforehand and want to blow off steam. It provides the opportunity to ground and become fully present. For instance, if someone has a sick child at home, the check-in allows them to get that off their chest so they can be more present in the meeting.

There are many ways to do a check-in that can be shorter or longer.

- The shortest version is: "What do you need to say in order to be fully present for this meeting?" You can go round the table and check who wants to say something. It is useful to educate a team on why you're doing this, so everyone has a better understanding of what you want to achieve.

- You can also choose to give people a couple of minutes to check their email and complete an urgent SMS or WhatsApp message. At the actual start of the meeting, we still recommend checking whether anything needs to be said to be fully present.

- In some meetings, you can perform a small mindfulness exercise. For example, focus on your breathing for a minute or listen to the fading sound of a singing bowl.

- You can also ask people how they feel right now. This can be in one word, one sentence, or a more free format, adding the sentence: "Take your time and know that we have more to do."

- There are also more structured check-ins. For example, in a meeting where people don't know each other well, you can ask people to share their name, role, years with the company, next holiday destination, etc. Including something personal breaks the ice and creates more safety. It is important here that everyone speaks, ideally voluntarily rather than in a fixed order. (Ask: "Who wants to go next?")

- You can also use the check-in to prepare the ground for the meeting. For example, by asking: "What do you expect of this meeting? What are your hopes and fears for this meeting? What do we need to have achieved when we leave this meeting?"

- Another powerful check-in question is to share a recent personal success and something that has been challenging. This reveals what people are working on and creates positivity and safety. In these cases, it is important to train people to keep their answers concise.

- You can be very creative with check-in questions (such as a metaphor describing your life right now, or your color today and why). The key is to understand why you are doing it and what you want to achieve.

- A powerful sequence we often use for the opening of a meeting is 1) check-in, 2) agenda of the meeting, and 3) designing the team and leader alliance. This may take some time but creates a powerful container for conversation.

The **check-out** is equally important. They can also be shorter or longer. The purpose is to provide an open space for people to say what is needed to complete the meeting.

- It could, for example, be: "What needs to be said right now to complete this meeting appropriately?" Or: "What is one word that describes how you feel right now?"

- A check-out can also be more extensive. For example: "What do you take away from this meeting?"

- It can also be a meeting evaluation: "What went well? What could be better? What do you want to celebrate? What has been marginalized/avoided in this meeting?"

Quotes from the interviews

"I have recognized that probably 75 percent of my job is really being a container for people, enabling them to do their work and being a motivator, coach."

- A DIRECTOR OF A HEALTH SERVICES AGENCY

"The role of the elders is to provide safety. You are climbing a mountain in the dark, and you know that the elders are standing at the foot of the mountain holding the space so that if you come tumbling down the mountain, the elders will bandage you and give you some wisdom and encouragement."

- THE OWNER OF A REGIONAL EXECUTIVE AND TEAM COACHING COMPANY

4. Amp-up positivity

Another powerful way to co-create Systems Inspired Safety is to build positivity. The two are highly correlated. Positivity is about acknowledging a person, a partnership, or a team. We are so trained in seeing what is not going well that we often forget to notice what is working, let alone express it. In our relationship systems training, we spend significant time on this topic and teach many positivity tools. This is not only to make the work environment more motivating and enjoyable, but also to build up the balance in the emotional bank account of the relationship. Dealing with relationship issues and difficult topics is so much easier and effective when this balance is positive.

We draw a lot on John Gottman's research on successful marriages. We already referred to his work in Chapter 8 when we discussed the toxins. Gottman found that 69 percent of relationship issues are perpetual. This means that you cannot solve them, so you need to find a way to deal with them. For example, in a partnership, someone is more orderly and structured while the other is more flexible and messier. This is not likely to go away over time, so you need to design around it and make it work together. It would be powerful to look at these differences with a positive lens: what is the strength of the quality that the other person brings? How could we create synergies?

Another of Gottman's findings is that healthy marriages have a **positivity/negativity ratio of five-to-one**. Barbara Fredrickson, a well-known researcher in the field of positivity, found something similar: the positivity ratio must be higher than three for flourishing rather than languishing. From a neuroscience perspective, our brains are wired for fight or flight. Negative feedback or experiences trigger either one of those. To overcome that, we need to have three to five times more positive experiences than negative ones.

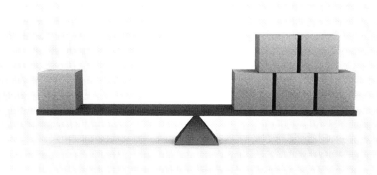

These findings are equally applicable to the workplace. If positivity is not part of the culture, building Systems Inspired Safety will be challenging. We, therefore, encourage you to develop a positive bias and be generous with your **compliments and acknowledgments**, both for individuals and the team/system. We notice in the field that these practices are often underrated. Many leaders/people operate from the principle that no news is good news and only speak up when things go wrong. This is really a missed opportunity. **Celebrations, positivity exercises, and championing** ("I believe in you; we can do this") are also powerful instruments to create positivity. It can also be created by "small" things like: **giving attention** ("How was your weekend?"), asking whether someone wants a cup of coffee, saying thank you, or giving a smile. These are all signs that you value the other person as a human being and that you are in a relationship together. They also create a sense of belonging.

Positivity is also strongly linked to having a growth mindset. The concept of growth mindset was coined by Carol Dweck and refers to people who believe that they can learn and improve and see failure as an opportunity to grow. This differs from people with a fixed mindset, who believe that capabilities are innate, fixed, and unchangeable.

Positivity work can be edgy. While most people crave recognition, it can be quite challenging in practice, both in terms of giving and receiving. Frank remembers that he had to adjust an acknowledgment exercise because it was too unsafe and vulnerable for the team he was working with to give each other public recognition. It needed to become a mingle, where people could exchange their appreciation more privately.

While we put a lot of emphasis on positivity, you must still honor the difficult moments or unintended impacts. The research honors the five-to-one ratio, but it is not suggesting that we can escape negativity, and we also are not advocating a five-to-zero ratio. It simply points to how best to mitigate negative impact and lead with positivity instead of constant negativity.

Sometimes, we hear that showing a lot of positivity will spoil people. In our experience, this is not the case. We do not think that you can give too much appreciation, provided you are genuine. The moment your positive remark is manufactured, people will spot it, and this is detrimental.

Emotions are contagious. Just as more toxicity will bring more negativity, more positivity will help to further improve the work atmosphere. In neuroscience, this is referenced as the work of "mirror neurons."

Practical applications: examples of positivity exercises

- Sit or stand in a circle and let each member say what they appreciate about this team and about a colleague in the room.

- In a circle, pair with somebody next to you. Take five minutes in this dyad and share in turns what you admire/enjoy/appreciate about your colleague.

- Let everyone tell the story about why they joined this company or team. Then together, retell the stories as an epic tale (Once upon a time…).

- Ask someone on your team to take a seat in the center of the room. Then encourage two people to come up and say something that they appreciate or admire about that person. The person in the seat can only respond by saying, "Thank you." After the acknowledgments are complete, the next person on the team takes a seat and the process repeats until every team member has been acknowledged.

This exercise can take some time, so please make sure you have enough time to get everyone through. Sometimes, more than two people want to express appreciation to someone. Don't let this happen as this may create some awkward inequalities. Also, we can only take so much appreciation so limiting to two people evens out the "appreciation playing field" and stops the group from being overwhelmed by praise.

Quotes from the interviews

"I organize an annual function where I invite everybody and recognize every single one. They all get a certificate."

- THE CHIEF OPERATING OFFICER OF A TRIBUNAL

"One of the things that I learned from the relationship systems approach is that no matter what, I want to keep that emotional bank with a positive balance."

- THE FOUNDING PARTNER OF A REGIONAL
COACHING AND TRAINING COMPANY

"I always had a positivity bias, even conflict that is happening from a positivity bias is a more productive conflict."

- A SENIOR AGILE MANAGER OF A GLOBAL CONSULTANCY

5. Be aware of your special position or rank as a leader

If you hold the outer role of leader in a team, be aware of the special position or rank that goes with it. It is easy to create fear unintentionally. Your role gives you certain privileges, including the power to make decisions, appraise performance, adjust pay, and influence career opportunities. This may create a force of gravity around you that causes people to behave differently. People may try to please you more and be more careful about what they say. And if it is not safe, they are probably not going to tell you, so you may think that everything is okay.

The **leader alliance** (see Chapter 6) is a great way of developing a productive relationship with your team. Take time to design it and review it regularly with an open and curious mind. **Also, feedback/feedforward rounds or anonymous 360 feedback** are great tools to provide you with vital insights on your leadership, including your ability to create safety.

Practical application: inviting and working with feedback

- Set up a session where you ask your team members to write on a sticky note something they appreciate about you as a leader, and on another sticky note, write something they would like you to do more or less. Then shuffle them in the team and read them out. Inquire and reflect on the input received and commit to one or two changes you want to make. Ask your team members to help you with these changes by giving you support and feedback.

- Discuss the outcomes of your 360 with your team. Share what actions you are going to take and ask them their support with realizing them.

Quote from the interviews

> *"It's a lifelong journey to keep being mindful and open to feedback. I encourage feedback."*
>
> - THE CEO OF REGIONAL COACHING AND TRAINING ORGANIZATION

ASSESS YOURSELF ON THIS COMPETENCY

- Rate yourself on a scale from 1 to 5 on the following beliefs and behaviors, where 1 means "I never do this," 3 means "I do this regularly," and 5 means "I do this all the time." [You can also use the digital assessment mentioned on the bonus page at the end of this book.]

- Add up the scores and determine how strong you are in this competency:

  - Between 10-20: you are becoming aware of this competency.

  - Between 20-30: you are developing skills in this competency.

  - Between 30-40: you are skilled in this competency.

  - Between 40-50: you are masterful in this competency.

- Now, determine what you would like to work on, using the ideas and practices of this chapter as input.

1. I actively invite team members to co-create a culture of safety, a space where people feel free to speak their minds.	....
2. I am aware of challenges in team member's personal life and honor the challenge of that.	....

3. I model vulnerability and creating from failure.	....
4. I support vulnerability in team members and stand for experimentation and learning.	....
5. I start a meeting with some form of check-in to get all voices in the room and get people present for the meeting.	....
6. I track the energy/emotional field to sense whether it is safe for people to speak up and invite the team to co-hold responsibility for that.	....
7. As part of creating safety in my team, I am aware when I speak first and last.	....
8. I actively invite positivity in my team.	....
9. I strive to catch team members at their best and share it with them.	....
10. I actively invite feedback on the impact of my leadership.	....

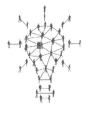

CHAPTER 10

THE BEING SIDE OF SYSTEMS INSPIRED LEADERSHIP

"My self-confidence has grown. It is just at a much deeper level, and it has sunk into a different knowingness. More of the being versus the doing."

**- AN ASSOCIATE DIRECTOR OF A
HEALTH SERVICES AGENCY**

1. Systems Inspired Leadership as a journey towards personal growth

The focus of this book is very much on the doing side of Systems Inspired Leadership. But we know there is also an impact on the being side, because being and doing are so interwoven in this space. In saying yes to this path, you are saying yes to vulnerability and daring to be brave. These notions came through in our interviews as well:

"For me, it was really a personal journey, yes great tools and skills, but it was fundamental for me to find out who do I choose to be and how I show up."

- A CUSTOMER OPERATIONS MANAGER
OF A MAJOR MULTINATIONAL

"You're learning these new techniques. But it's really working on you as a human being. It has led me to a greater level of maturity, because of the inner work that you go through.

- THE SENIOR AGILE MANAGER OF A GLOBAL CONSULTANCY

"The relationship systems approach really changed my life, both from a professional and private standpoint. From a human being standpoint, because you cannot divide it. For me, it is a way of being and influencing my whole life."

- A CUSTOMER CHANNEL DIRECTOR OF
A GLOBAL TECHNOLOGY COMPANY

The being side is about who you are and how you view yourself, others, and the world. It is about your own personal development and mindset. Many leaders in our interviews shared how they had grown as a person, not only as a professional, from attending the relationship systems training and adopting Systems Inspired Leadership.

"I'm less worried that my input is not seen as professional enough, and I'm able to be more vocal. That is a big transformation for me."

- AN ASSOCIATE DIRECTOR OF A HEALTH SERVICES AGENCY

"The systemic perspective, the wisdom of the system made me much more robust in my relationships with colleagues and leaders. I'm less intimidated."

- THE OWNER OF A LOCAL COACHING COMPANY

"The relationship systems approach helped me trust that unknown things could happen that would be useful and beautiful. It also helped me to see more deeply that negativity and tension are revealing important things that can be used and remediated and built upon to help the system become healthier and achieve objectives better. So, it's just given me more depth as before and I think that has also let me be more confident and calm."

- THE FINANCE DIRECTOR OF A HEALTH SERVICES AGENCY

We believe that there are many elements in the Systems Inspired Leadership approach that will support and challenge you in your growth as a human being. For example, to live the systems inspired rule ("everyone is right... partially") requires significant self-awareness and a willingness to be open to influence. It requires you to step away from judgment and react-ing and step into curiosity and empathy. This also applies to the notion of Deep Democracy that holds that every voice has wisdom. Are you able to do this? Are you able to refrain from judgment? Metaskills play an import-ant part here. They are the bridge between doing and being. Also, seeing people as human beings rather than as instruments to get the job done, and building right relationship, for many, is a fundamental shift.

Adopting this way of modern systems thinking widens your horizon. You are becoming more aware that we are all interconnected and interde-pendent and that listening to all the voices and receiving input from the collective does not only create a different measure of efficacy, it also creates the much-needed sense of belonging within the team and enterprise. As a result, leaders, as well as team members, are more open to collaboration for the benefit of all stakeholders involved, rather than favoring some of them. This is also where Relationship Systems Intelligence becomes crit-ical. The emphasis on Relationship Systems Intelligence takes us beyond the awareness of what is happening in myself and others, and it extends to the awareness of the relationship system itself and the ability to create from it and leverage its intelligence and creativity.

Systems Inspired Leadership can be seen as a journey to deepen your own wisdom, your personal evolution in service of not only yourself, but the larger whole. In the research on adult development, this has been identified as the ability to grow "vertically." It will enable you to better deal with the increased complexity in the world and move up on the stages of adult development, as described in the model of Kegan and Lahey on the next page.

Stages of Adult Development

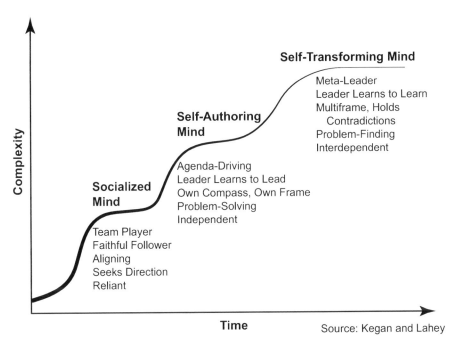

Source: Kegan and Lahey

Exploring the being side of Systems Inspired Leadership is a broad field and could merit many chapters. Given that the focus of this book is on the doing side, we will limit ourselves to some aspects only. For us, the being side of Systems Inspired Leadership is very much tied to adult development and the three intelligences: Emotional Intelligence, Social Intelligence, and Relationship Systems Intelligence.

In the remainder of this chapter, we will deepen this by exploring how to be in right relationships with the system of "me," the system of "we," and the system of "IT." "Right" in this context is not about the simplistic right or wrong. It refers to being in a relationship of integrity and honoring values within yourself, with others, and the larger whole. This is a critical path in human evolution.

Welcome to the journey!

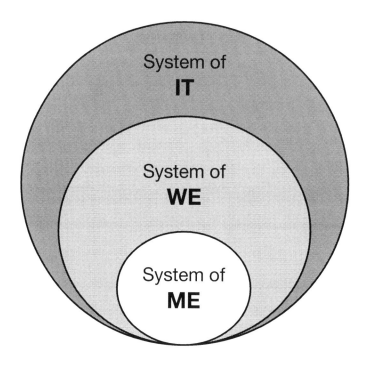

2. The system of me

You, as a human being, are a relationship system as well. "Self" is the first system. In this case, the parts aren't necessarily other people but the members of your inside team as described by one of our senior faculty, Cynthia Loy Darst, in her book *Meet Your Inside Team*. Biology sums up the physical parts. Did you, for example, know that the human body comprises thirty trillion cells that work (mostly) harmoniously and productively together without a "chief" directing them? This exhibits the systemic principle of interdependence. In organizational terms, we can liken that to a distributed leadership model. Then there are the psychological elements, the different parts or selves that make up who you are, some known, others not. And often, there are opposite parts or voices. For example, a part of you wants to complete an important task and another part of you wants to take a break. Both live in you, so how to deal with them appropriately?

Discovering your own inner system and being committed to its continued evolution is a big and lifelong endeavor. For every individual, there is so much to discover: who you are, your strengths and values, your passions, what gives you fulfillment, what holds you back, your traumas, your secret selves, your marginalized parts, your unwelcome parts, your limiting beliefs, your triggers, your fears, etc.

Emotional Intelligence plays an important part here: are you aware of your own emotions and feelings, and are you able to master them without suppressing them or projecting them onto others? Do you know how to be in right relationship with (the various parts of) yourself? Individuation and evolution of personal selves have been the study and practice of multiple disciplines for centuries and have evolved in concepts such as EQ.

Ultimately, vertical development is the path of personal evolution as we navigate and create awareness of the complexity of all the different voices within us. When you consider that, notice how difficult it is for us to connect or become aware of all those voices—skillful or not—unless we are in a relationship with someone or something outside of us. We need others to discover ourselves!

We look at the system of me in the same way as we look at other systems. The principles of **Relationship Systems Intelligence** apply here as well. You are unique and naturally creative and intelligent. We hold that all voices within you count and have wisdom. If there are internal conflicts, this is, in effect, emergence in action. What is trying to happen? What is wanting to come to the surface?

Adult and leadership development is a process of evolution; it is the natural propensity of human beings to grow and evolve. How are you holding that need for personal evolution and vertical development and not only the challenges associated with that but also the opportunities? How can you be conscious and intentional about your personal growth?

For many people, the fact that this approach acknowledges all parts of you is a big relief. It is not about avoiding, marginalizing, or suppressing. It is about honoring all the different voices and inner roles making up the complexity of what makes you uniquely *you*! Given that, how can you design your internal alliance, showing respect for all voices and aligning what wants and needs to be collectively achieved? This work is very much linked to healing. Healing is about becoming whole, integrating all parts of the personal system.

If you are interested to explore this further, we recommend the previously mentioned book *Meet Your Inside Team* by Cynthia Loy Darst. It says: *"When your inside team is working together, everything can be great, and life is wonderful. But when your Inside Team is not aligned you can feel stuck, anxious, confused or judge and beat up on yourself.*

We encourage you to develop right relationship within yourself and build and grow your inside team, as part of your natural growth as a human being and leader. The path of Systems Inspired Leadership is compromised in the absence of this.

Practical application

Consider something that you find challenging (e.g., having a difficult conversation or giving a presentation to a big audience). Who are the various players in your mind that voice a point of view about this (e.g., "yeah let's do this" or "this will be a failure again")? Map them on a piece of paper and consider the truth or wisdom of each of them. Then design a team alliance (see Chapter 6) focused on how you want to be together with these different voices from within, as you tackle the challenge.

Quotes from the interviews

"When we think systemically, the first system is self.
I can think of myself as a system that has not one role/
voice but many."

- THE CEO OF A GLOBAL COACH TRAINING
AND CONSULTING COMPANY

"So from the me-perspective, I needed to own my dark side,
own my scars, own my ugly side, but owning them means
living with them sometimes, not always comfortably, but
acknowledging that they serve a purpose, not just to me but
out there in the world too."

- THE CEO OF REGIONAL COACHING
AND TRAINING ORGANIZATION

3. The system of we

This refers to a relationship between you and one or more persons. We = I + You. It could be a partnership or friendship, a family, a team, an enterprise. There are three aspects to explore here: how to be in right relationship with yourself as well with the other person. And how to be in right relationship with the 3rd entity (so the relationship system itself).

Being in right relationship with yourself is the place of **Emotional Intelligence** that we discussed above (see system of me).

Being in right relationship with the other is the place of **Social Intelligence.** It is about discovering the "land" or environment or experience of the other. The other person is "the same but different." What are those differences? What is attracting you? What is irritating you? What are you allergic to? It is growing your ability to stand in some else's shoes and stay non-judgmental, curious, and open to influence. Interestingly, in meeting others, you get to know yourself better as well. The differences make you aware of what is "normal" for you. And the irritations and allergies may say more about yourself than the person involved. The point of being in a relationship might well be to help you grow and understand yourself better.

The seven Metaskills we highlighted in Chapter 6 (heart, Deep Democracy, playfulness, respect, collaboration/partnership, curiosity, and commitment) are powerful ways to build right relationship with others.

Being in right relationship with the 3rd Entity—the relationship itself—is where **Relationship Systems Intelligence** becomes relevant. As mentioned before, RSI states that whatever is happening to any individual is personal, AND it is also an expression of the system. Individual profile, bias, psychological disposition, etc., will shape how that is expressed by the individual, and the essence of what is expressed also lives within the system.

What is wanting to happen in the relationship itself—beyond the viewpoints of the individuals inhabiting the relationship? What is the purpose/ goal of the relationship? What if you belong to the relationship instead of it belonging to you? What does it know that you do not? What does it need from you? What wisdom does it have for the two or more of you that are occupying it? This allows you to listen to, and create from, the relationship.

An example of the magic of the 3rd entity in action is the way Frank met his wife Vera. Following a series of less successful relationships, friends arranged a blind date for him. He initially resisted as it did not fit his picture of romantic love and autonomous self. Still, they met, and it worked out magically. There was a wonderful and easy connection between them with much love and pleasure. How could it be that something that proved so difficult with others was so easy here?

It became even more magical when having children came up. This was not so much on Frank's mind. But when Vera raised it, he intuitively knew it made sense. It would be good with her. And she had a similar feeling—as if the relationship entity was calling them to make this happen. She got pregnant the moment they said yes to it; was this a coincidence or good luck? It's hard to say, of course, but sometimes, it feels as if the relationship has been waiting for the individuals to finally step into it, as if something much bigger has been doing the "dreaming" for it for the longest time. We are not used to this way of thinking. Still, there are many examples like this when you start looking for them. What "meaningful coin-cidences" are happening in your relationships? And what "children" want to be born from them?

To be in right relationship with the 3rd entity is to be in direct com-munication with the Relationship System itself, and to be open and listen to what it sees, feels, needs, and wants. And then seriously consider what new information might be available and actionable from *that*. As someone said in the interviews, *"It is about our ability to hear the things that want to come through us."*

This equally applies to systems of we that are bigger than two people, like a family or team. Peter Hawkins, a well-known scholar in the field of systems thinking, says, *"It is the purpose that creates the team—not the team that creates the purpose. The purpose is already out there in the world waiting for a team to respond."* In other words: the 3rd entity of any relationship is "dreaming up" the players it needs into place. It has been waiting for you and can now express itself through you.

Practical application

1. Identify someone who irritates you.

    Explore what is irritating, the characteristic. What is the quality of it, and how is this living in you? How could it be useful too? Now, imagine that you can step into the space of the relationship between the two of you. What information do you get from that perspective? What advice or information does "IT" have for you?

2. Imagine someone at work you have a good relationship with. What is the purpose/goal of your relationship? What is uniquely possible through this relationship? What does this relationship want you to do? What does it need from you?

Quotes from the interviews

"This work has taught me to see and feel what others are going through and to be able to empathize, even if I don't agree, I can still empathize, and I see more now the impact that I have on the 'you' part."

- THE CEO OF A REGIONAL COACHING
AND TRAINING ORGANIZATION

"This awareness relates to giving myself a fraction of a second more to reflect on whatever is going on, rather than instantly reacting to things. Sort of like checking: Where am I? What things are coming my way? What is happening in the relationship? And then opening up to the possibility of being curious rather than instantly getting into reaction."

- THE FOUNDING PARTNER OF A REGIONAL
COACHING AND TRAINING COMPANY

"Understanding that everything we see in someone else is a projection, and it often says more about me than about the other person. And we are handing each other masks all the time, which are projections, so how do we handle that? How do we accept the ones that fit us and reject the ones that are not?"

- THE CEO OF REGIONAL COACHING
AND TRAINING ORGANIZATION

4. The System of "IT" (the larger whole/ecosystem/cosmos)

This notion focuses on systems that are bigger than the system of we and more anonymous, the "IT." It shifts the gaze from the team to the bigger enterprise, from government to country, from individuals to community, from system to ecosystem, from people to humanity, the planet, even the cosmos. It also includes new and big ideas, dreams, and longings that want to manifest themselves in the world. How can you be in right relationship with that?

It is about the subtle interplay between yourself and the bigger 3rd entity. This is where your calling as an individual becomes important. What do you want to create in the world? What is the legacy you want to leave behind? This is quite a magical space. Joseph Jaworski, a renowned leadership scholar, talks about connecting with *"Source,"* the *"infinite potential enfolded in the universe."* Connecting to this Source *"leads to the emergence of new realities—discovery, creation, renewal, and transformation. We are partners in the unfolding of the universe."*

And while it may be easier to consider the voice of the relationship itself in smaller systems, it is extremely relevant to also lift the gaze and evolve the ability to include the larger systems surrounding you. To hear all voices of the system and access the voice and information from the ecosystem itself is critical. It is only when we transcend the individually or politically motivated voices that new information and viewpoints will emerge. This will enable the players in ecosystems to find alignment in how to move forward and optimize the interests of all stakeholders involved rather than prioritizing the interests of just a few.

An interesting example is the impact of the COVID-19 crisis. In addition to the undeniable loss, grief, uncertainty, and fear, it also brought, for many, a moment to pause and reflect and an opportunity to let go of old habits. The images of the blue skies over Beijing and the view of the Himalayas from India made us think—as if Mother Nature invited us as a species to reflect on what we were doing and what we could learn and do individually and collectively.

Another example is the creation of ORSC. Marita co-founded this with Faith Fuller, and the way they started was quite extraordinary. Both of them were working with Joanna Macy, a thought leader in the Gaia movement, which preceded much of the work around what we now know as the global climate crisis. Marita was in a consulting role with Joanna on the West Coast of the USA as Faith was working with her on creating an organization on the East Coast to house this movement. A meeting of global thought leaders occurred in the San Francisco Bay area driven by this emerging initiative.

Faith and Marita held key roles in this auspicious meeting, which was also the first time that they met in person. Both attest, from looking in the rear-view mirror, that this was the initiative that their 3rd entity had "co-dreamed" and was waiting for. The rest is history. It became not only the birth of what would become the Naropa Institute in Colorado, but also the genesis of Organization and Relationship Systems Coaching (ORSC) and CRR Global. It was their 3rd Entity that created the ORSC program and founded CRR Global. They have also been in a committed relationship for over two decades.

In hindsight, it might be seen as a cosmic invitation through an outsider to come together and create something special. And this apparently required a mixture of the personal and the professional. It required the personal commitment to weather storms, disagreements, and resistance. Once they committed to the relationship and the work, the next steps started to show up, like breadcrumbs to follow. One of their favorite sayings is that "out of every argument or disagreement, a new workshop was born!" It was not about Marita and Faith having figured this out; it was a response to something bigger. The work just happened, as if they were conduits for it. Like an old Indian saying, "I thought I was planning, and all the while I was blown across the sky by a great wind."

In a way, this book was created similarly. There was the sense that it needed to be written. Frank remembers that he sent the idea to Marita in an email in December 2018 and within 1.5 hours he got her answer: "But of course!" As if we were channels for something bigger.

And it is a place of paradox: on the one hand, it is where the most authentic self comes to the surface. On the other hand, it is where you are a servant, serving something bigger. Our purpose and a much larger universal purpose play together, and that is what creates evolution. It is a true reflection of the magnificent work described by Arnold Mindell in his book *The Dreammaker's Apprentice* in which he holds that we are both the "Dreammaker" and the "Apprentice." What if the 3rd entity (or the relationship Itself) is the "Dreammaker" of both the dream and the apprentices?

From this perspective, Systems Inspired Leadership could be defined as **being a masterful conduit for what an (eco-)system wants or needs to achieve**. It is about serving multiple and ever bigger 3rd entities. Ultimately, **Systems Inspired Leadership is about accelerating human evolution**.

Systems Inspired Leadership is About Accelerating Human Evolution

The Ability to Connect with Self, Others and the Larger Whole

Practical application

Reflect on an urge you have to create something in the world that is bigger than you.

Step 1: What is this urge? What is the big dream you have about it? Speak to the dream: what does it say? Have a conversation with the dream rather than just talk about it. Take turns being you and being the dream. What is trying to happen from that conversation that provides you with direction and new insight? Create action from that.

Step 2: Who are you called forth to follow through on this? Is it your partner, a good friend, a respected colleague? Discuss it with this person. What insights does this conversation bring you? What is a bold step you could take in the desired direction?

Quotes from the interviews

"I think we experience ourselves as being called forth to do something, being a conduit for something that needs to emerge. How do I become a support for the evolution of the entire system? How do I not get in the way?"

- THE PRESIDENT OF A GLOBAL COACH TRAINING
AND CONSULTING COMPANY

"There is more and more awareness that there is something so much bigger than us; it's so tied to that deeper life purpose."

- THE CEO OF A GLOBAL COACH
TRAINING AND CONSULTING COMPANY

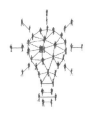

CHAPTER 11

IMPLEMENTING SYSTEMS INSPIRED LEADERSHIP

"For the sustainability of this work and for its acceptance, it needs to be part of the organization. My advice is don't do it alone, get a cohort of your colleagues to do it together."

**- LEADERSHIP DEVELOPMENT LEAD OF
A GLOBAL TECHNOLOGY COMPANY**

1. Systems Inspired Leadership is a different way of leading

In the interviews, we heard many stories about the positive impact of Systems Inspired Leadership. Interviewees were enthusiastic about what it brought to them, both personally and professionally. At the same time, they acknowledged that it was not always easy. It required personal growth and commitment, which can be uncomfortable and challenging. And it also required skillful maneuvering in organizations that are not used to this approach.

Systems Inspired Leadership relies on getting information from the system and its members and to co-create with the system from that. While there is enough research and evidence that we are moving away from top-down leadership, this still proves difficult for many larger global companies and governments with strong and more rigid structures. Establishing good ground conditions for change has become a norm that many strive for by using input models and obtaining information from stakeholders as well as employees. However, holding leadership as a role that—beyond the designated outer role—belongs to the system is still relatively uncommon.

The answer does not necessarily need to come from the leader. It can also come from the members of the team or even from the system itself (the 3rd entity concept, as described in Chapter 5). This shared leadership model has emerged in recent years and is currently finding more and new expressions. It is challenging on both sides of the experience—for leaders as well as for team members. Team members have been educated and brought up to be "followers" and not responsible for making decisions. In this new leadership paradigm, they can often feel uncomfortable and disturbed because they are not used to participate in this way. That in itself can set the emerging Systems Inspired Leader up for falling back into old habits of "telling what to do."

We are currently seeing many organizations steering away from the strict hierarchical approach and adopting a more agile way of working and using self-managing and distributed leadership teams. These approaches map well with Systems Inspired Leadership, which is very well suited to complex and rapidly changing environments. As someone said, *"If we can begin to equip more and more people with this way of thinking, it changes organizations and it changes the world, it really does."*

And let us add some nuance to this. It is not about throwing away the old. It is about integrating a new approach into your leadership. It is about including what is good from the old to transcend it in new, evolutionary ways. In the end, Systems Inspired Leadership is about expanding range and roles. Its core value is *to create from the system, trusting that the answer is already there and waiting to be revealed.* And, at times, other approaches may be needed, depending on what is required in an instance. For example, taking decisions and holding people accountable are important leadership tasks, as well as having difficult conversations in case of non-delivery. Sometimes, you need to adopt a more directive approach, e.g., in a crisis or when an urgent deadline must be met. Having said that, the danger in a crisis is that it is easy to fall back hastily into the old top-down pattern rather than slow down and ask what is trying to happen.

Below, you find what leaders in our interviews found challenging about implementing Systems Inspired Leadership and some suggestions about what can be done about it.

2. Key challenges of implementing Systems Inspired Leadership

2.1 Overcoming personal barriers as a part of your personal growth

The personal work associated with leadership development applies to Systems Inspired Leadership. Becoming a good leader starts with leading self. This is a very personal journey, depending on factors like personality, background, experience, and organizational culture. For example, some leaders found it challenging to move away from command and control and take on a more systemic approach. Some had to become less nice, set more boundaries, and speak up. Others found it difficult to slow down and to reflect, particularly in stressful situations. For others, it was the shift in focus from task/process to people/relationships or from content to emotions/feelings. Everyone has their own personal journey, and these changes are often hard as they require you to move away from an approach that worked well and brought you a lot.

Possible action: find a coach or trusted colleague to discuss and work this to enable you to evolve in your own journey.

Quote from the interviews

"I used to think, 'Get out of here, leave me alone.' Now I say to myself, 'The relationship is the work.'"

- A DIRECTOR OF A HEALTH SERVICES AGENCY

2.2 Balancing task and relationship

People often have a natural preference for being either task-focused or people-focused. To be effective you need both. Given where society is right now, Systems Inspired Leadership has a bias for the people/relationship side, but there is a focus on achieving results as well. In the interviews, the polarity between the masculine and feminine came up very often. Both qualities are needed, and they need to be deployed flexibly, like a fluid dance, depending on the situation. The same applies to related polarities like hard and soft, rigor and compassion, or guiding and holding. It is about expanding your range so that you can do what is required in a specific circumstance.

Possible action: get to know your system. If you are task-focused, become the Systems Inspired Leader who will call on your team members who are naturally people-focused to be your allies, and together, you birth the solution. You may not have all the needed qualities in all situations. The collective knowledge of your team and the balcony view of the voice of the system itself *will* have it. Leverage that!

Quote from the interviews

"A lot of the profiles I see are very one-sided, either relationship or task, and it's hard for people to do both."

- A LEADERSHIP DEVELOPMENT LEAD
OF A GLOBAL TECHNOLOGY COMPANY

2.3 Switching hats and roles

As a Systems Inspired Leader, you often have a "holding" and facilitating role. You reveal, ask questions, and enable emergence. At the same time, your role requires you to make decisions, give direction, appraise and sometimes dismiss people. This is not only challenging for yourself but also for the people around you.

Possible action: what helped many leaders was to be very clear about which hat they wore at any given time: e.g., mentor, facilitator, coach, line manager, or decision-maker.

Quotes from the interviews

"There is still a point where I think as a leader you need to prune the vineyard, sometimes you still have to make these tough calls."

- A SENIOR AGILE PROGRAM MANAGER
OF A GLOBAL CONSULTANCY

"I frequently use the "colleague" hat. That place of being able to occupy the seat of colleague and referencing a time in my life or career where I struggled and had difficulty. This really helps to create connection and grow systems inspired safety."

- THE CEO OF A GLOBAL COACH TRAINING
AND CONSULTING COMPANY

2.4 Making your own voice heard

Linked to the above, some were so deep into the facilitator/coach role that they found it hard or forgot to make their own voice known. This happened, for example, frequently with HR professionals who were asked by their CEO to facilitate and coach the leadership team. It is important to address this as your voice needs to be heard. You are part of the system and hold vital information.

Possible action: for a period, hand your facilitator/coach hat to a team member and speak from your experience as a *team member*. In a situation like this, it might be useful to literally vacate your chair, let the designated facilitator/coach step into it, and sit and speak from a different seat!

Quote from the interviews

"I was pushed by the management team to facilitate every single workshop in the company. But as a result, I felt that my voice was not heard. So for the last two years, whatever we are doing as the management team, we are outsourcing it."

- AN HR DIRECTOR OF A RETAIL ORGANIZATION

2.5 Educating/enrolling the organization

There are many challenges at the organizational level as well. How can you introduce and embed this in the organization when the culture is very different? Systems Inspired Leadership is a different approach that takes time to master. It is not plug-and-play. Not everybody will be convinced and enthusiastic, and not everybody will be willing, ready, or capable to make the change. And the results may not be immediately visible (remember the sailboat analogy in Chapter 3: systems often change in seemingly small steps). And that is challenging when there is relentless pressure to perform and get things done.

Possible action: make Systems Inspired Leadership the core of a culture and/or leadership development program. The key is that the top leaders join as well, to create a common language and develop role models.

Quotes from the interviews

"You show them the why and they say: 'Interesting but come back to business; we have more pushing things to do.'"

- A SALES EXECUTIVE OF A GLOBAL ENGINEERING COMPANY

One of the most challenging issues is persuading the system to consistently invest in this kind of training. So in start-ups, you are all the time in a roller coaster; you are always understaffed, either you are before or around a fundraising round or you are after."

- AN HR EXECUTIVE OF A DIGITAL SCALE-UP

2.6 Language

There was also a lot of discussion about what language to use. In our relationship systems training and applications, we employ a specific jargon (like most mental models) that may not appeal immediately to everyone. As in medicine, law, etc., these concepts explain the theoretical model for all professionals in the discipline. The language the dentist uses to you as the patient in the dentist chair is very different from the language they use for their assistant making notes or handing instruments. In this book, we used a selection of the relationship systems vocabulary. We introduced concepts like relationship system, Relationship Systems Intelligence (RSI), 3rd entity, Metaskills, emotional field, voice of the system, and edge. How can you use these words in a way that attracts people rather than alienates them?

Possible action: meet the system where it is, use language that it can relate to, and gradually introduce the above language. More and more people are becoming aware of a new language as the concepts and research are readily available on the internet. And more and more, we hope for this to become part of everyday language as a new era arrives.

Quote from the interviews

"I'm really using very, very normal conversational words to bring forward some of the concepts."

- A SENIOR AGILE MANAGER OF A GLOBAL CONSULTANCY

3. Key practices to implement Systems Inspired Leadership successfully

3.1 At the Individual level: practice, practice, practice

The only way to master the competencies required for Systems Inspired Leadership is to practice them. For example, it takes time to learn to lift your gaze and see things systemically, to experience and work with the emotional field, to "see" edge behaviors, and to deal with your own uncertainly and triggers. What helps is to see failure as an important step in prototyping change and growth. Find yourself a buddy or support team (many countries have regular ORSC alumni gatherings). Set development goals for yourself and invest in your personal growth (e.g., minimum of two weeks of training annually).

3.2 Educate your team

Enrolling your team is also powerful. Explain to them why you do what you do, introduce the language, give examples, and show the bene-fits. Do it regularly, with a light touch, preferably in the moment, and repeat it often enough for the message to sink in. And deepen this with the people who show interest and have energy for it. In this way, you can easily create a guiding coalition.

3.3 Role modeling

This is very powerful; people see you doing it and notice the impact. They may not immediately be able to articulate what you do, so educate them. They are probably going to copy you, so it is a great way of building capability in the organization. Ideally, the CEO or head of the organization adopts and promotes this approach as well. This will impact the culture and makes embedding so much easier. One of the most important—and challenging —role modeling is to own mistakes and failures and to share learning from them.

3.4 Make it the core of a culture and/or leadership development program

This is by far the most effective way to embed Systems Inspired Leadership in your organization. We can attest that many organizations globally have done so effectively. Ideally, the program has a time span of at least one year to ensure that the change is sustainable. Engage in training and ensure that conditions are created where the new approach can be practiced and implemented. The shelf-life of efficacy through training alone is rather short, and the top leaders must join as well. This is invaluable in creating a common language with which people can support each other and create a culture shift. As part of these programs, it is advisable to build internal capability as well, so train people who can support their colleagues in their development. This can be people in HR as well as others. We also see that Systems Inspired Leadership is often integrated with the agile way of working. These approaches are very complementary and help to build organizations that are adept at fast change and high complexity.

Practical application

- Create a plan to develop further as a Systems Inspired Leader. What do you want to focus on? What resources do you need? Who could support you?

- Think about your team. What could you do to build more capability? How well do you role model Systems Inspired Leadership? How often do you educate your team?

- Think about your organization. What would be a good way to introduce Systems Inspired Leadership? What are the key stakeholders? Who could be the early adopters?

Quotes from the interviews

"It is so hard to be that kind of solo pioneer because then you become really pushy, and I know that myself because I was the only person doing it. It's lovely to have a community around you that has the language, who you can build upon, work with, fail."

- A LEADERSHIP DEVELOPMENT LEAD OF
A GLOBAL TECHNOLOGY COMPANY

"It takes time you know. It takes time to sit down and speak to someone, have a conversation with your team members. And we know that it is an investment because it bears fruits. It is a marathon we are after."

- A MANAGING DIRECTOR OF A REGIONAL COACHING
AND TRAINING COMPANY

CONCLUDING THOUGHTS

"My motto or my purpose is to change the world one system at a time, and I'm very conscious that we have an impact and that that impact has a ripple effect."

- A CEO OF REGIONAL COACHING AND TRAINING ORGANIZATION

We hope you found this book useful and enjoyable. Since systems are in a constant state of emergence, we love for you to notice what is emerging in you. How are you called to apply these insights and bring them into the world? Your intention and impact may initiate so much more. We believe we all take part in the emergence process of humanity and this is your ripple!

Our hope is for a broad adoption of Systems Inspired Leadership in organizations. We believe this will change organizations and the world. We hope that it will resonate with established leaders who want to lead differently, having experienced that the current way of leading is not working anymore. We also hope that young leaders will embrace this approach and that it will help them to accelerate their personal development. Actually, it would be great if all employees received access to this material and gained from it, as each of us is a leader. We hold that leadership is a role of the system, and everyone has a role to play!

Looking broader, technology will likely become an important aid in revealing the system to itself. The time-lapse between idea and reality will be shortened significantly so that feedback loops will become clearer much faster. (It won't take us fifty years to discover that the oceans are full of plastic.) Technology can become a powerful help in revealing what is happening or trying to happen in large ecosystems. We already know of organizations that gather stories in their ecosystems and feed them back in creative ways to provide a picture of what is happening, and in this way, they help people and systems to make conscious choices.

We hope this will impact democratization processes as well. Currently, politics have become rather unhealthy, with so much emphasis on what divides people rather than what unites them. There is so much polarization, which has resulted in so many stuck systems. Alignment work is an important go-to here. What can we align on? What might we be able to create from that? Promoting role fluidity by encouraging people to start taking different roles/perspectives, and wearing different "hats," will help to unlock systems and to get the information flowing again. This all requires consciousness and a willingness to change.

More scientific research on Relationship Systems Intelligence and the supporting principles and competencies would be most welcome. We feel this is an important field of study and more scientific work will help deepen the understanding and provide an empirical basis for its relevance and impact.

We would be delighted for the key notions of Systems Inspired Leadership to be brought into our education system, including primary and secondary education. The world will be changing so fast in the coming years that the ability to learn and create from emergence will become so much more important than gaining actual knowledge. The Systems Inspired approach contains many useful ingredients for helping young generations with this, particularly around dealing with complexity and the unknown, the interdependent nature of our world, and the realization that everyone's voice has wisdom and a right to be heard.

John Renesch, another great scholar in the field of systems thinking, argues in his book, *The Great Growing Up* that humanity is still in the adolescence phase of development, being self-centered rather than taking responsibility for all life forms. We hope that this book will serve as another piece of help to bring humanity into adulthood and convert the speed of change into the speed of evolution.

GLOSSARY

3rd entity	Refers to the powerful relationships between people in a system and highlights the unique qualities, personality, character, spirit, and culture of a relationship system. It is the relationship system itself as a living organism with its own unique wisdom and personality separate and different from its players.
Alignment	Refers to finding the common goal or interest in a relationship system and creating action from that.
Conflict	Refers to opposing views, perspectives, and opinions in a relationship system. Conflict is seen as a systemic event, a signal that change is needed in a system and that something new is trying to emerge. Conflict is the engine for change, provided it is productive rather than toxic.
Deep Democracy	The belief that all voices in a system are important and have wisdom, including the marginalized and unpopular ones.

Designing the Team Alliance (DTA)	Refers to designing together the "being" or "social contract" of collaboration in a specific meeting or around a specific task. It creates the culture needed to execute the task at hand. It is about how to be together while working on an initiative, and it should not be reduced to "who will do what by when." It fosters collaboration and increases creative retrospectives in service of becoming more effective as a team and building a culture of efficacy.
Edge model	A powerful lens to track and create conscious awareness of the impact of change or impending change in a relationship system. The edge divides the current and established identity (the known) and new identity (the unknown).
	Edge as such refers to the no-man's land separating that which an individual, team, or organization identifies with at any given moment versus that which they do not. The latter could be what they are becoming or forced to become or what they have marginalized or disavowed. Inevitably, there are emotional obstacles that people or systems need to cross to get access to this new identity.
Emergence	The natural tendency of relationship systems to evolve as an expression of their potential. Emergence brings the new to the surface. It occurs when a system gets properties or behaviors its parts do not have on their own. They only emerge when the parts interact in a wider whole.

Emotional field	The type of energy within a relationship system as it evolves moment by moment. It is often not spoken about despite always being present and sensed, and, therefore, it is a rich and often neglected source of information when working with systems.
Emotional Intelligence (EQ)	The ability to be aware of your own emotions and taking responsibility for actions flowing from those.
Metaskill	Refers to the feeling quality that brings your skills to life and makes them more effective. It is about the stance, attitude, and intention you bring to your actions. What is the energetic impact you want to make on the system? The outcome is to create an intentional energetic field within which the work is done.
ORSC	Organization and Relationship Systems Coaching (ORSC). ORSC is a powerful team and partner coaching model providing tools and skills with which to focus and reveal the web of connection—or relationship system itself—as the client or stakeholder. It is informed by RSI and it informed the Systems Inspired Leadership model.
Relationship system	A group of interdependent entities with a common focus or goal.

Relationship System Intelligence™ (RSI)	Refers to the ability to interpret an individual's experience (and that of others) as an expression of the system. The experience is personal and also belongs to the system. It focuses on the relationship system itself (rather than on the individuals/elements in that system) and enables the ability to create from the system and help it grow and evolve collectively. It is theoretically underpinned by five important principles.
Social Intelligence (SI)	The ability to accurately read the emotions of others, and the capacity to empathize.
System	See "Relationship system."
Systems Inspired Leadership™ (SIL)	The ability to create and lead from the system, trusting that the answer is already there and waiting to be revealed. Rather than directing the system, Systems Inspired Leaders facilitate emergence. They work with and rely on the system to give birth to what is trying to happen. They hold leadership as a role of the system and grow shared leadership at all levels in the organization.
Systems Inspired Safety	Ability to co-create a space where people feel comfortable to speak their truth and share their vulnerabilities. It lives in a Systems Inspired Culture where team members believe they will not be punished or humiliated for speaking up with ideas, questions, challenges, or mistakes. The ability to hold and open up a creative space.

System of "IT"	Refers to the collective whole and is bigger than the system of we. It shifts the gaze from the team to the bigger enterprise, from government to country, from individuals to community, from system to ecosystem, from people to humanity, the planet, even the cosmos. It also includes new and big ideas, dreams, and longings that want to manifest themselves in the world.
VUCA	Volatile, uncertain, complex, and ambiguous; characterizes the context of the twenty-first century.

APPENDIX 1: ORGANIZATION AND RELATIONSHIP SYSTEMS COACHING PROGRAM (ORSC)

Systems Inspired Leadership draws heavily on the teaching and practices of Organization and Relationship Systems Coaching (ORSC). ORSC is the flagship program of CRR Global, a well-known international Coach Training School based in the USA, specializing in working with relationship systems such as teams and organizations. ORSC is a powerful coach program that puts systemic interdependence and relationship systems in the foreground. Over the last two decades, CRR Global has trained over 20,000 practitioners worldwide, ranging from the Americas to Asia, from Europe to Africa, from the Middle East to Australia, and demand is growing.

The ORSC curriculum comprises three parts: the fundamentals (two days introduction course); the intermediate series (four sets of three days, covering various aspects/dimensions of working with relationship systems); the certification (eight-month part-time program for further deepening the material and becoming masterful).

The following concepts have been directly derived from the ORSC curriculum:

- 3rd entity

- Alignment work

- Designed team and leader alliance

- Informal constellation

- Lands work

- Relationship Systems Intelligence (RSI)

- Sensing and working with the emotional field

APPENDIX 2: FORTY WAYS TO READ AND WORK WITH THE EMOTIONAL FIELD

NOTE: your tone of voice is really important here. It needs to be neutral and should refrain from judgment.

Questions to ask about the emotional field

1.   What just happened?

2.   What is here now?

3.   What is in the laughter?

4.   What is it like (to experience that)?

5.   What is the weather within the team right now?

6.   What is the emotion within the team right now?

7.   What is the atmosphere in the room at the moment?

8.   What are you aware of for this team at the moment?

9.   How would you describe the team spirit right now?

10.   Wow, what is that?!!

11.   Is there an elephant in the room right now?

12.   How does/did this land?

Language to describe an emotional field

__NOTE: When using any of these, it is always useful to have person or group elaborate or explore what you just noticed and ask them for different or better language. Articulate what you sense. Do not interpret.__

13. I am sensing/noticing/seeing/hearing/feeling …

14. It feels like the sun just came out (or other weather types).

15. There is a lot of camaraderie here.

16. There is a feeling of hope here.

17. I feel there is a strong sense of connection as you say that.

18. I sense a lot of warmth here.

19. I sense some lightness/playfulness/laughter right now.

20. There is a spirit of collaboration right now.

21. There is a strong commitment between all of you.

22. Feels like you are making progress.

23. It feels kind of bumpy.

24. It feels there is a thunderstorm going on.

25. I sense some disconnect.

26. I am noticing distance between you.

27. I am noticing something like tension/fear in the space.

28. Feels like there is fatigue within your team today.

29. It feels kind of dull/flat.

30. Now the argument is getting hotter.

31. It is clear how painful this is for the team.

32. Now there is silence.

33. I notice that everyone is looking down (or whatever signal is happening). What is here?

34. The temperature just changed here.

35. Noticing lots of confused faces right now.

36. Lots of thought processing going on.

37. Everyone is going really fast.

38. I can feel the ripples of what just happened.

39. It is like (metaphor).

40. That feels like—I do not know what it is. You describe it.

Adapted from "101 Ways to Read the Emotional Field" by Maddie Weinreich.

APPENDIX 3:
120 POWERFUL METASKILLS

Metaskills refer to the feeling quality that brings your skills to life and makes them more effective. What is the desired culture you want to seed the room with while you are working on a task or outcome? What is your intention? What is the atmosphere you want to create in the room that will best serve the system? What is the energetic impact you want to make on the system? What attitude or "come from place" will best serve the difficult (or fill in the blank) conversation? There is power in reflecting and rehearsing how you want to enter a conversation or meeting.

Below, you will find a list of powerful Metaskills. The ones in **bold** are the seven Metaskills that are particularly useful for building right relationship. *Note that we are using "relationship" in its fullest sense as the collective noun for all relationships. Hence the word relationship without the plural "s."*

List of powerful Metaskills

1	Abundance		**30.**	**DEEP DEMOCRACY (*)**
2	Acceptance		31.	Delight
3	Admiration		32.	Determined
4	Affirmation		33.	Disturbance as an Ally
5.	Aliveness		34.	Disturber
6.	Appreciation		35.	Diversity
7.	Assertive		36.	Ease
8.	Balance		37.	Easy command
9.	Beauty		38.	Effective
10.	Boundlessness		39.	Efficient
11.	Brisk		40.	Effortless
12.	Care		41.	Empathy
13.	Cautious		42.	Empowerment
14.	Centered		43.	Energetic awareness
15.	Challenging		44.	Entertaining
16.	Clarity		45.	Enthusiasm
17.	Coachlike		46.	Equanimity
18.	**COLLABORATION /PARTNERSHIP**		47.	Everything is workable
19.	Collegial		48.	Excitement
20.	**COMMITMENT**		49.	Experimenting
21.	Compassion		50.	Exploration
22.	Composed		51.	Failing is OK
23.	Confident		52.	Fascination
24.	Connection		53.	Fatherlike
25.	Courage		54.	Flexible
26.	Creative		55.	Fluid
27.	**CURIOSITY**		56.	Focus
28.	Daring		57.	Forgiveness
29.	Decision Making		58.	Friendship
			59.	Fulfillment

60.	Generosity	91.	Patience
61.	Gentleness	92.	Peace
62.	Giving 100%	**93.**	**PLAYFULNESS**
63.	Gratitude	94.	Positive
64.	**HEART**	95.	Presence
65.	Honesty	96.	Productive
66.	Hope	97.	Pure
67.	Humility	98.	Realism
68.	Humor	99.	Relaxed
69.	I am OK	**100.**	**RESPECT**
70.	Inspiration	101.	Result oriented
71.	Interested	102.	Rigor
72.	Joy	103.	Serious
73.	Keep things moving	104.	Simplicity
74.	Learning	105.	Space
75.	Light touch	106.	Spontaneity
76.	Lightness	107.	Stillness
77.	Love	108.	Strength
78.	Magic	109.	Support
79.	Motherlike	110.	Tenderness
80.	Neutral	111.	Thoroughness
81.	No Bullshit	112.	Trust
82.	Non-attachment	113.	Understanding
83.	Non-judgment	114.	Vital
84.	Not-knowing	115.	Vulnerable
85.	Objective	116.	Warmth
86.	Openness	117.	Warrior
87.	Open to Influence	118.	Welcoming
88.	Partnership	119.	Wisdom
89.	Party	120.	Wonder
90.	Passion		

(*) Believing that all voices in a system are important and have wisdom

APPENDIX 4:
CONFLICT PROTOCOL

Conflict Protocols are useful guidelines that effective teams develop to manage conflict constructively. Below is a model for creating that. Please write down your answers to the questions below and discuss and review them with your team.

Think about your ideal team

How would that team handle conflicts and disagreements? Jot down a few points.

....

....

....

....

What are some behaviors you want to happen when conflict occurs?

For example: give constructive feedback, speak to the person directly rather than complaining about them behind their back, get all the stakeholders together rather than triangulating, etc.

....

....

....

....

....

What are some things you do not want to happen when conflict occurs?

For example: toxic behavior, hostile gossiping, triangulating, breaking or reopening agreements, etc.

....

....

....

....

It takes six to nine months to change a behavior.

How will you hold one another accountable for following these agreements? What will you do if someone breaks an agreement?

....

....

....

....

What will you do if someone breaks an agreement?

....

....

....

....

BIBLIOGRAPHY

Buckingham, M. & Coffman C. (1999). *First Break All the Rules.* Pocket Books.

Carnegie Mellon University (2010). "CMU, MIT and Union Study Shows Collective Intelligence of Groups Exceeds Cognitive Abilities of Individual Group Members." Carnegie Mellon University, Oct 2010.

Damasio, A.R. (1994). *Descartes' Error: Emotion, Reason, and the Human Brain.* Penguin Books.

Deloitte (2019). Deloitte 2019 Global Human Capital Trends Report. "Leading the Social Enterprise: Reinvent with a Human Focus." *Deloitte Insights* Magazine.

Deloitte (2020). Deloitte 2020 Global Human Capital Trends Report. "The Social Enterprise at Work: Paradox as a Path Forward." *Deloitte Insights* Magazine.

Duhigg, C. (2016). "What Google Learned From Its Quest to Build the Perfect Team." *The New York Times* Magazine Feb 2016.

Dweck, C. (2006), *Mindset: The New Psychology of Success.* New York: Random House.

Edmondson, A.C. (2019). *The Fearless Organization.* John Wiley & Sons.

Fredrickson, B.L. (2009). *Positivity: Top-Notch Research Reveals the 3-to-1 Ratio That Will Change Your Life.* New York: Crown.

Fridjhon, M., Fuller, F & Rød, A. (2014). Relationship Systems Intelligence: Transforming the Face of Leadership. CRR Global Website. https://crrglobal.com/resources/downloads/

Gallup (2021). "U.S. Employee Engagement Rises Following Wild 2020." Gallup's Workplace Management Practice February 2021.

Goleman, D. (2006). *Emotional Intelligence.* New York: Bantam Dell.

Goleman, D. (2007). *Social Intelligence: The New Science of Human Relationships.* Bantam.

Gottman, J. & Silver N. (1999). *The Seven Principles for Making Marriage Work New York*: Three Rivers Press.

Hawkins, P. (2019). *Systemic Coaching: Delivering Value Beyond the Individual.* The World Business & Executive Coach Summit.

Herder-Wynne, F., Amato, R. & Uit de Weerd, F.J. (2017). "Leadership 4.0. A Review of the Thinking." Research Report. Oxford Leadership.

IBM (2019). IBM Study: "The Skills Gap is Not a Myth, But Can Be Addressed with Real Solutions." IBM News Room, Sept 2019.

Jaworski. J. (2012). *Source: The Inner Path of Knowledge Creation.* Berrett-Koehler Publishers.

Kegan, R. & Lahey, L.L. (2009). *Immunity to Change: How to Overcome It and Unlock the Potential in Yourself and Your Organization (Leadership for the Common Good).* Harvard Business Review Press.

Kübler-Ross, E. & Kessler, D. (2014). *"Grief and Grieving: Finding the Meaning of Grief Through the Five Stages of Loss.* Simon & Schuster.

Lewis, M. (2008). *Inside the No: Five Steps to Decisions that Last.* Deep

Democracy (Pty) Ltd.

Lieberman, M.D. (2013). *Social: Why our brains are wired to connect.* Crown Publishers/Random House.

Loy Darst, C. (2018). *Meet Your Inside Team: How to Turn Internal Conflict into Clarity and Move Forward with Your Life.* Team Darst.

Mindell, A. (2001). *Riding the Horse Backwards: Process Work in Theory and Practice.* Lao Tse Press.

Mindell, A. (1995). *Sitting in the Fire: Large Group Transformation Using Conflict and Diversity.* Lao Tse Press.

Mindell, A. (2002). *The Dreammaker's Apprentice: Using Heightened States of Consciousness to Interpret Dreams.* Hampton Roads Publishing Company.

Mindell, Amy. Metaskills (1994): *The Spiritual Art of Therapy.* New Falcon Publications.

Renesh, J. (2011). *The Great Growing Up: Being Responsible for Humanity's Future.* Hohm Press.

Rød, A. & Fridjhon, M. (2020). *Creating Intelligent Teams.* Amazon.

Scharmer, O. & Kaufer, K. (2013). *Leading from the Emerging Future: From Ego-System to Eco-System Economies Kindle Edition.* Berrett-Koehler Publishers.

Snowden, D.J. and Boone. M.E. (2007). "A Leader's Framework for Decision Making." Harvard Business Review, November 2007.

Stanford Graduate School of Business (2011). "Alan Mulally of Ford: Leaders Must Serve, with Courage." YouTube video.

Tate, W. (2009). *The Search for Leadership: An Organizational Perspective.*

Triarchy Press.

The Guardian (2012). "Unilever's Paul Polman: challenging the corporate status quo." *Guardian*, 24 April 2012.

Wheatley, M. (1994). *Leadership and the New Science: Learning about Organization from an Orderly Universe.* Berrett-Koehler Publishers.

Zenger, J.H and Folkman, J. (2009). *The Extraordinary Leader: Turning Good Managers into Great Leaders.* The McGraw-Hill Companies.

ACKNOWLEDGEMENTS

We want to acknowledge and send kudos to the many thought leaders and change-makers we are associated with—those who spent many hours with us in the trenches, creating from systemic emergence.

First, we'd like to express our deep appreciation for Arnold and Amy Mindell, who influenced our work over decades of collaboration and training.

We also want to express our appreciation to the many other thought leaders in the field of systemic leadership and coaching, particularly Peter Hawkins, Peter Senge, Marshall Goldsmith, Margaret Wheatley, Daniel Goleman, John Gottman, and Otto Scharmer.

Closer to home, in the circle of CRR Global, without the dedication and commitment to this work that so many of you—faculty, global partners, alumni—brought to our training and development processes, this book would not exist. A special thanks to Faith Fuller, Anne Rød, Cynthia Loy Darst, Mish Middelmann, Klaus Lombardozzi, and Jennifer Campbell. You have sat with us since the inception of our work. For that, we will always be grateful.

In addition, this book was significantly informed by the input and experiences of the interviewees who told us firsthand what it is like to be a Systems Inspired Leader. These clients, partners, and alumni provided empirical evidence that helped to sharpen the theory and practice of what we speak to in this book whilst validating our core concepts and ideas. In particular we want to mention: Aylin Yazcan, Camiel Gielkens, Cesar Fentanes, Chris Powers, Elfie Zaid, Fahmeeda Khan, Farhann Ali, Floyd Carlsson, Frank Wiewel, Gerold Hake, Gill Dore, Jutta Graefensteiner, Keiko Muramatsu, Klaus Lombardozzi, Leslie Morse, Lia Polderman, Linda Berlot, Lisa Warhuus, Marelize Bosch, Mike Holton, Mish Middelmann, Nairy McMahon, Nati Treister-Goren, Rachel Barouch, Rebecca Gebhart, Seda Nufuscu, Tuere Anderson, and Zuzi Sochova.

We also want to acknowledge the people who provided valuable feedback on the manuscript. In particular we want to thank Katie Churchman, Hajni Sagodi, Fionnuala Herder-Wynne, Leslie Morse, Cara Antoine, Gabriëlle Kalkwijk, and Jennifer Pernfuss.

We must also recognize our life partners for their ongoing support. In particular, we want to shine the light on Vera Uit de Weerd-Kramer. How many weekends were absorbed by the writing of the book and how many Tuesday evenings were influenced by the calls with Marita?

Once all is handled, no book will appear unless there is a publisher and editor to help facilitate launching. Many thanks to Howard VanEs and his team at Let's Write Books, Inc.—your support has been outstanding!

For everything we do and engage in, we have been an apprentice of something bigger that wanted to express itself through us. If we honor this, we will be acknowledging very differently. Not one person, not two people wrote this book. It too was created by a bigger system. We are grateful to be its conduits. And for its ongoing expression, we pass it on to others to build upon and further evolve…

ABOUT THE AUTHORS

This book brings two streams together. There is the extensive corporate experience of *Frank Uit de Weerd* who could clearly see the power and need of the relationship systems approach for leadership in modern organizations. And there is the extraordinary experience of *Marita Fridjhon*, CEO of CRR Global, who is not only a thought leader in the field of team coaching and systemic evolution, but also as a mediator, consultant, and team coach in global corporate environments. She created the foundation for RSI and Systems Inspired Leadership and invented the term Systems Inspired Leadership. Both are passionate about bringing Systems Inspired Leadership into the world and the evolution of leadership. It is through their relationship system that this book was born.

Marita Fridjhon, born in South Africa and based in the USA, is co-founder of CRR Global. Marita has an academic background with degrees in medical and psychiatric social work as well as family systems therapy. Growing up in South Africa during the apartheid era and being a faculty member at Cape Town University profoundly impacted her and created the basis of exploration in systemic change. That became the driver to embark on cross-cultural research, including two years on the Amazon River and work in Brazil, Perú, Columbia, the British West Indies, and Puerto Rico, to name but a few.

The outcome of these experiences provided training and focus on corporate, NGO, and government work using mediation, process work consulting, and coaching. Together with her partner, Faith Fuller, she founded the international training and consulting business CRR Global, home of the legendary ORSC curriculum. As CEO of CRR Global, Marita heads up a global distributed leadership team with partners in fourteen different countries and a global training faculty. She also develops curriculums and provides team coaching.

Marita is a highly sought-after global speaker and is the lead author of the article "Relationship Systems Intelligence: Transforming the Face of Leadership" and co-author of the book Creating Intelligent Teams. You can contact her directly via **www.crrglobal.com** or by emailing **info@CRRGlobal.com**.

 *Frank Uit de Weerd,* a Dutchman living in the Netherlands, is an organizational psychologist and trusted advisor and coach for leaders, teams, and organizations. He is a senior faculty member of CRR Global, trainer of the ORSC approach, and supervisor of their certification program. He builds on more than twenty-five years of experience in a large, corporate organization (Royal Dutch Shell), where he made an international career in human resources with assignments in the Netherlands, UK, Belgium, Gabon, and Malaysia.

Since 2015, Frank has been working as a trusted advisor and coach for leaders, teams, and organizations. He is an inspiring speaker and co-author of the Dutch book "Leading Innovation" and of the article "Leadership 4.0: A Review of the Thinking." You can contact him directly via **www.aoidosleadership.com** or by emailing **info@aoidosleadership.com**.

You can also visit **www.systemsinspiredleadership.com** or send an email to **info@systemsinspiredleadership.com**.

BONUS

Get a **FREE** Systems Inspired Leadership Profile to find out where you are on your leadership journey and how much progress you are making. Also benefit from podcasts and the latest news about Systems Inspired Leadership.

Visit: www.systemsinspiredleadership.com

Here is an example of the Profile:

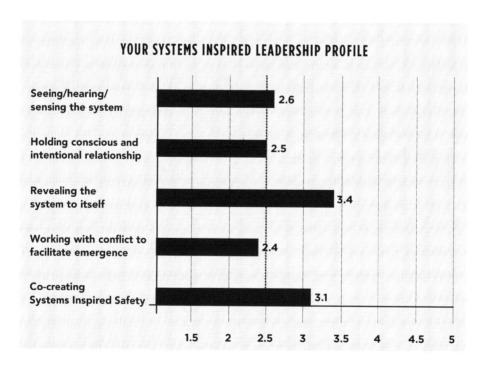

YOUR SYSTEMS INSPIRED LEADERSHIP PROFILE

Seeing/hearing/sensing the system	2.6
Holding conscious and intentional relationship	2.5
Revealing the system to itself	3.4
Working with conflict to facilitate emergence	2.4
Co-creating Systems Inspired Safety	3.1

1.5　2　2.5　3　3.5　4　4.5　5

Made in United States
Orlando, FL
02 November 2023

38531379R00139